"I love Brandon Bowers. H .... planters are my heroes. I especially love the leadership principles that
he shares in his new book *Rise Above the Lies*. It's so easy to get
caught up in thinking that kills momentum. Brandon shows us
how to renew our minds with truth."

Greg Surratt
Founding Pastor, Seacoast Church
President, ARC, Association of Related Churches

"Brandon Bowers is one of the best young leaders I have ever
dealt with. If you were to see his team and their heartfelt unity
and effectiveness, then you would know he is much more
than just an author. Brandon uses his leadership skills to lead
his church towards making disciples in relationship as Jesus
modeled. He is a practitioner and not just a theorizer. He is
definitely a leader you should become familiar with. God is using
him, and he can help you as a culture builder in whatever setting
you are leading in."

Jim Putman
Founding & Senior Pastor, Real Life Ministries

"Brandon Bowers is one of the wisest, most humble young leaders I know. He's an old soul with his finger on the pulse for leading the next generation. Get ready to be challenged and encouraged as you embark on a new chapter of leadership."

Grant Skeldon
Next Gen Director at Q Ideas

"Brandon Bowers is an immensely gifted leader. Every page of this book flows out of the reality of his life journey of obedience to the call of God. *Rise Above the Lies* is so factually on target and practical in application."

Dr. Donald J Wilton
Senior Pastor, First Baptist Spartanburg

"The challenges of leadership can often feel overwhelming. On top of that, we as leaders all wrestle with lies about our skills, our relationships, and our situations. The only way to defeat these lies is to destroy them with God's truth, which is exactly what Brandon Bowers does in this powerful read. This book will help you to personally grow in your faith, your influence, your passion, and your leadership."

Dr. Jack Graham
Senior Pastor, Prestonwood Baptist Church

"This book is a must read for anyone currently in or aspiring to be in a leadership role. Read this book and learn how to positively impact lives and leave a legacy."

Chris Singleton
Inspirational Keynote Speaker
Former Professional Athlete

"*Rise Above the Lies* offers both insightful and practical leadership principles that are solution-oriented and designed to drive you towards greater success. No matter what field you're currently leading in, this book is one that you can't afford to miss!"

Luke Yetter
Director, Relational Discipleship Network

"What I love about Brandon is that he says what we're all thinking. It's hard to diagnose the lies that we aren't willing to admit we're buying into, but in *Rise Above the Lies*, Brandon not only accurately assesses the lies leaders tell themselves, he gives us powerful truths from God's Word to help us heal from the wounds those lies have inflicted upon us. This is one of the best leadership books I've ever read. It will not only make you a better leader, it will make you a whole one."

Luke Lezon
Pastor at Lifebridge Church, Leader of Quay

"These truths are spot on and will help you avoid common pitfalls that hijack many leaders. With a transparent posture, and an easy to engage story-telling style, Brandon shares valuable leadership lessons from his journey in planting and growing a church. I will be strongly recommending this book to the church planters we serve at Exponential."

Todd Wilson
President & CEO, Exponential

EXPOSING THE LIES THAT LEADERS BELIEVE &
EMBRACING THE TRUTHS THAT WILL MAKE YOU SUCCEED

RISE
ABOVE THE
LIES

BRANDON BOWERS

Copyright © 2021 by Brandon Bowers

All rights reserved. No part of this publication may be reproduced, distributed, or transmitted in any form or by any means, including photocopying, recording, or other electronic or mechanical methods, without the prior written permission of the publisher, except in the case of brief quotations embodied in critical reviews and certain other noncommercial uses permitted by copyright law. For permission requests, write to the publisher at the address below.

Fedd Books
PO Box 341973
Austin, TX 78734

www.thefeddagency.com

Published in association with The Fedd Agency, Inc., a literary agency.

Unless otherwise noted, all scripture quotations are from the Holy Bible, New International Version®, NIV® Copyright © 1973, 1978, 1984, 2011 by Biblica, Inc.® Used by permission. All rights reserved worldwide. "New International Version" and "NIV" are registered trademarks of Biblica, Inc.®. Used with permission.

Scripture quotations marked (NASB) are taken from the New American Standard Bible® (NASB), Copyright © 1960, 1962, 1963, 1968, 1971, 1972, 1973, 1975, 1977, 1995 by The Lockman Foundation. Used by permission. www.Lockman.org

Scripture quotations marked (MSG) are taken from THE MESSAGE, copyright © 1993, 1994, 1995, 1996, 2000, 2001, 2002 by Eugene H. Peterson. Used by permission of NavPress. All rights reserved. Represented by Tyndale House Publishers, Inc.

ISBN: 978-1-949784-54-1
eISBN: 978-1-949784-55-8

Library of Congress Number: 2020921585

Printed in the United States of America

First Edition 21 22 23 24 / 4 3 2 1

Ashley …
for always believing in me.

Brailey, Bryson, Brinkley & Brooklyn …
you inspire me, motivate me, and make me better.

Awaken …
we're changing the world together.

CONTENTS

INTRODUCTION

Leadership is influence, nothing more, nothing less.
—John C. Maxwell, *The Maxwell Daily Reader*

In my early twenties, my dream was simple: change the world. With an undergraduate degree, a beautiful and successful fiancée, and a ministry position at one of the largest churches in the United States, I was eager to devote myself to learning how to lead people to the best of my ability while also leveraging any influence I had to make a positive difference in this world. My intentions were as pure as gold and my ambition was off the charts. I was finally surrounded by great leaders with even greater opportunities before me. At the ripe age of twenty-three, I had the world at my fingertips and the audacious faith to believe that God would do amazing things in and through me as a leader. I had so much to learn.

Most leaders begin here.

A dream. A goal. A vision. A desire to be part of something so much greater than themselves. It is the young lawyer who longs to launch a practice that will see justice prevail for the overlooked and underprivileged. The entrepreneur who truly believes his product will enhance the lives of millions of people. The artist whose music will unite cultures and build bridges that connect people from all around the globe. The teacher who wants to devote her life to shaping the minds of the next generation. The athlete putting in thousands of unseen hours and working tirelessly to leave a legacy of a champion while also leveraging her platform for social justice. The millennial starting a nonprofit organization to change the broken culture of his beloved city. The coach who loves winning, but loves developing young men into successful husbands, fathers, and community leaders even more. The list goes on and on and on.

As you follow your dreams and find success in your field, the influence that follows will propel you into leadership. People will begin looking to you and depending on you. Teams will develop, and they will need to be led. Vision must be cast to create clarity and culture. Systems will need to be formed. The vision once planted as a seed in your heart will begin to produce an abundance of fruit in your life. This means more people. More processes. More meetings. More responsibility. More decisions. More problems. More everything. The more convoluted things get, the higher the chance your dream will begin to dwindle in light of the not-so-glamorous details it takes to lead well.

In order to be a successful leader, you can't just be a dreamer; you have to also do. When I started out in ministry at twenty-three, my dream was to change the world. But without details, specifics, systems, processes, and meetings, my dream was just that: a dream. It's the building and the mojo of everything that leads to a legacy, a purpose fulfilled. Once I got more specific and action-oriented about my dream, I was able to build something incredible: a thriving three-campus church where I get to lead and inspire people every day.

There is no shortage of advice or guidance on how to become a better leader. I have personally read many leadership books and scoured through countless articles. Much of my own development has come from these resources. For that, I am grateful. However, you need to know that this book is not that. Throughout my role as a leader, I've seen great success and great failure, terrifying valleys and stunning mountain tops. I have gathered information from my own experience as well as the experiences of others, and I've built a framework to help leaders gauge where pride is causing them to buy into the common lies every leader will face. When we fight against the lies that creep up during leadership and work at the virtues every great leader possesses, we will experience success beyond our wildest dreams and live a fulfilling life. This is the stuff nobody tells you starting out but has the potential to destroy you along the way. There is great danger in believing things that can compromise your convictions while poisoning your passion. This is a discussion about the feelings you don't share, the struggles you don't see, and the tension you can't ignore. This is an honest examination of what you believe as a leader. About yourself. About your team. About your dream.

Becoming a leader starts with a dream. A vision. But what distinguishes a leader from a great leader is how they will respond to the lies surrounding leadership when they pour their whole heart, soul, and schedule into something.

It starts with a dream, a desire to get better. You believed it. Yet, along the way, you heard the lies and maybe even believed them. Now your dream has dwindled. Your faith has faded and you don't know what to do. This is about getting your dream back. This is about fighting for the faith that it took to begin while finding the fortitude to continue moving forward. This is about developing the seven attributes that set great leaders apart from the masses and identifying the lies that keep you from experiencing success in those areas.

Your best days as a leader are before you and success is straight ahead. Building unshakable vision and unprecedented success starts with figuring out what lies you believe.

CHAPTER 1

THE EVOLUTION OF A LIE

You will know the truth, and the truth will set you free.

—Jesus Christ (John 8:32)

In February of 2017, Kyrie Irving, the Duke University standout, five-time NBA All-Star, and point guard for the NBA champion Cleveland Cavaliers, shocked the world. It wasn't a buzzer beater. It wasn't a triple-double. It wasn't a trade between teams. In fact, it wasn't anything to do with basketball or sports at all. It was just a statement he made:

"The earth is flat."

It was absurd. As early as the sixth century BC, philosophers and mathematicians discovered and proved that the earth is spherical. And now we have nifty satellite images that verify their claims. There have been countless discoveries that prove the earth to be round.

But what if it is all a lie?

See, what made the Kyrie Irving earth-is-flat episode so absurd was that he ignored millenia of scientific discovery and cold, hard facts. Something we know to be true—that the earth is, in fact, round—he refused to believe. He believed a lie. This multi-millionaire professional athlete who had the GPA and SAT score to get into Duke University had the audacity to ignore the mountain of evidence that the earth is spherical and defend this lie. Repeatedly. Kyrie later admitted he got sucked into a rabbit hole of a conspiracy theory through a series of bogus YouTube videos. Regardless, he was clearly pushing and promoting an obvious lie. How does that even happen?

It always seems ludicrous when someone believes and defends such a bold-faced lie. Yet becoming defensive is only natural when you can't see the lie for what it is. The root cause of this denial and defense is called *pride*. Pride is the foundation upon which every failure and lie about leadership is built.

Defend at all costs.

Don't admit to fault.

Refuse to hear people out.

Attain more power or position.

Rebel for the sake of personal gain.

This is how the very first lie was born.

The creation account found in the Bible tells the story of God creating the very first people, Adam and Eve. They were a perfect couple with the world at their fingertips. A beautiful garden. A plethora of animals. Fruits and vegetables aplenty. Just imagine a beautiful oasis with warm sunshine, cool air, birds chirping, and a river with the subtle sounds of rushing water—like a scene from one of those Sandals Resorts commercials that is so perfect it appears to be fake. Adam and Eve are newlyweds, completely naked, hanging out in paradise. It doesn't get much better than that. They had it all. Life was good. Until it all came crashing down.

We're told that Satan appeared in the form of a serpent one afternoon and asked just one question of Eve: "Did God really say, 'You must not eat from any tree in the garden?'"[1] Eve replied with the clear instructions that God had given to her and her husband. They could eat of any tree they wanted except one: the tree that was in the middle of the garden, the tree of knowledge of good and evil. What happened next changed history.

"'You will not certainly die,' the serpent said to the woman. 'For God knows that when you eat from it your eyes will be opened, and you will be like God, knowing good and evil.'"[2] The serpent twisted God's words into a lie. He exploited the humans' pride. "It's not for your protection that you should stay away from that tree, but for the prevention of becoming like God." Eve, poisoned by pride, bought the lie that Satan was selling. She took the bait. She actually believed it.

Eve proceeded to make her way to the middle of the Garden of Eden. She grabbed an apple from that forbidden tree and she took a bite. Then she found her husband, Adam, and shared the sinful treat with him. They immediately felt shame and saw each other differently. They felt the need to cover up and sewed some fig leaves together for clothing. Then, desperately, they scrambled to hide their failure from God. They were ashamed, afraid, and ended up running for their lives, only to have God eventually find them hiding under a rock. All hell had broken loose, not over an apple, but over a lie.[3]

Freedom became fear.

Paradise turned to paranoia.

Relationships were ripped apart and trust was gone.

All because of a lie.

This same scene plays out every day in boardrooms, locker rooms, conference rooms, and offices all around the world. Leaders inevitably find themselves embracing lies that have either been told to them or that they have created along the way. These lies shape their behavior and lead them to fear, paranoia, shame, and isolation. Business relationships begin to suffer, networking relationships become strained, and interpersonal relationships fall apart. The stress and pain of these failures cause leaders to question their abilities to lead well or even survive the game they are playing. They begin to doubt their competency, second-guess their calling, and maybe even contemplate stepping out altogether. Many a leader has lost their company, been fired, forfeited their family, or even taken their own lives. The threat is imminent and the danger is real. Lies are from the pit of hell.

Lies have a negative connation for a reason. They are misleading, deceiving, and honestly, downright evil. They spew forth from the media, the government, and across social media platforms by the minute. We tell them. We believe them. We endorse them and even share them. White lies. Half-truths. One side of the story or just straight gossip. They are everywhere. Unfortunately, lies are an unavoidable part of our everyday lives.

You would think that, by now, we would have figured out how to notice and negate many of these lies. As human beings with intellect, rational thinking, and the ability to reason, you would think we would be more aware. However, the truth is that many of the lies we believe are much subtler than we think. They are unseen and unspoken. They are hidden, and they lurk in the shadows and secrets of our lives. These lies develop as defense mechanisms to avoid the same kinds of pain filed away from our past or as prescriptions to fight the poison in our past. They manipulate our minds and warp our well-being while we don't even recognize that it's happening. We begin to live and lead according to what we believe, not even realizing what we believe is actually false and informed by pride. We establish and lead businesses, companies, teams, and ministries without thinking about why or how we do certain things. We operate out of assumptions and find ourselves too busy to stop and think. There is little time for inspection, less time for reflection, and no time for introspection. And without introspection, the lies just keep their control over us.

Lies will exist for as long as the earth is round. But if we are aware of the ways they show up and take root in our lives, then we will be able to meet those lies with truth. Truth existed long before the first lie; it is what we must keep going back to in order to renew our minds and strengthen ourselves for the course ahead.

When we meet lies with the truth and values God has entrusted us with, we will be able to guard ourselves against the lies that try to limit our passion, confidence, purpose, drive, and ambition. All of these values can be twisted, just like the serpent in the garden with the apple (*Clue* reference, anyone?), and turn into lies that lead to your destruction. The key is to temper these values with humility; otherwise, pride will distort them. And pride, as we know, is the sin that destroys even the best of leaders.

There is an old saying that clearly highlights this principle: "Pride comes before a fall." Pastors, leaders, coaches, and teachers have quoted this truth for hundreds of years. Its roots can be traced all the way back to an Old Testament king named Solomon. In the book of 1 Kings, King Solomon reigned over the nation of Israel for forty years during what is known as "The Golden Age" of the Jewish nation. He honored God and led his people to live according to God's commands. His accolades include powerful military dominance and financial prosperity, bringing him more wealth than anyone who had ever lived. He was successful, powerful, rich, and famous. Bottom line, Solomon wanted for nothing. He spent his days lounging under palm trees by the pool with women (*lots* of women), piña colada in hand, and not a worry in the world. Think Las Vegas casino, resort-style living … but you own the house. That was King Solomon in his prime. His life was good.[4]

Yet most scholars believe it was during this time, at the peak of his outward success, that he wrote the following words: "Pride goes before destruction, a haughty spirit before a fall."[5]

While Solomon was able to lead the nation to its highest pinnacle of success, his pride became the poison that also led the nation into the depths of despair. Pride leads you to believe you are somehow exempt from the principles you preach. It can blind you from seeing the deficiencies of your own character while inviting you to dive into destructive behaviors. What happens in Vegas does not stay in Vegas; it stays in your heart. While it is one of the most tragic stories in all of human history, we would do well to learn from a leader like Solomon so our story has the chance of turning out much differently.

The good news for you is that your best days as a leader lie ahead. You have chosen to read, reflect, and recognize whether or not these lies have taken root in your own mind. If you have been leading for any substantial period of time, these lies have affected you and those under your influence. You have the opportunity to identify these lies and then decide how you will change course to overcome them. You have the ability to pause and process why things are the way they are and what it will take to make them better. Your teams will get stronger. Your company will thrive again. Your passion will be refueled and your vision will be renewed. Your relationships will be restored and your future will flourish.

CHAPTER 2

PASSION IS POTENT

The visionary lies to himself,

the liar only to others.

—Friedrich Nietzsche[1]

Lie #1: No one cares as much as me.

In the summer of 2012, I took the largest step of faith I had ever known. I was leading as the College and Young Adults Pastor on the executive team at First Baptist Church of Spartanburg, South Carolina, a church with a membership of over 7,000 people. Under the incredible leadership and direction of Dr. Don Wilton, this church took a chance on me as a young, fiery kid fresh out of college. Though I was still trying to figure out what faith and leadership really looked like, I was passionate and excited to be in an environment where leadership was valued and modeled extremely well. Despite my questioning of all kinds of traditions and refusal to wear anything other than jeans to worship services, they patiently developed me into a man of God and trained me to be a leader who understood what influence meant and what lasting impact looked like. It was there that I learned to be a husband, a father, and a man who lives with conviction and compassion. I was serving under a great leader, I was married to the girl of my dreams, and my wife and I were raising three awesome kids in a close community of friends and neighbors. Life was good in every way imaginable.

However, I began to sense God leading us to make a move to Charleston, South Carolina. I consider Charleston my home. It's where I grew up, went to college, met my wife, and got married. It's also where I began my faith journey and spent the early days of leading my ministry. While I was convinced that God was leading us toward a move, I was incredibly nervous about the unknowns of the situation. *Where would I work? What church would I serve? How would we start? What part of the city? How will I make money? Am I crazy?* It had been over ten years since we had graduated college and left Charleston, so the thought of moving back to start from scratch was terrifying. Through many conversations and much godly counsel, my wife, Ashley, and I knew what we had to do. We were convinced God was leading us to move and start a new church—to leave our megachurch of thousands of people and go start a church from scratch. Beginning membership? Five, all with the last name Bowers.

I know it sounds crazy. And the truth is, it *was* crazy. On some days, looking back, it still doesn't even make sense to me. Yet, I've found that God works in the midst of crazy. It's called *faith*. He loves it and honors it. In fact, the Bible says, "Without faith it is impossible to please [God]."[2] I felt it was our only option because the faith I follow tells me that when God says to do something, you do it. Who cares if it makes sense? It's following a promise and not a feeling. So on January 30, 2012, I walked into my pastor's office and formally resigned from my position at First Baptist Church Spartanburg. The bear hug and encouragement I received from Dr. Wilton that day was a treasure I will never forget. I had made the decision. There was no turning back.

We moved at the end of summer. The last week of August, to be exact. It was a natural time of transition for us and the small team that was moving with us. It also happened to be the hottest time of the year to pack up a house and a U-Haul. Late August in the South serves up regular temperatures in the mid-nineties with a guaranteed 100 percent humidity, so moving that time of the year made about as much sense as everything else on the journey. Thankfully, we had the help of many friends who packed furniture, mattresses, toys, and way too many clothes into a couple of U-Haul trucks. We loaded up, hit the local IHOP for breakfast, and started down Interstate 26 with nothing more than a God-given dream and hearts full of determination. Even now, I remember driving the truck out of the parking lot that day with increased blood pressure and excitement. I can still feel the faith it took to keep driving, and I can hear the prayers I was so desperately praying alone in the cab of the truck. So much fear, but so much faith. And so much that I didn't even know was on the way.

Once we arrived in Charleston, I immediately began working a full-time job with a small startup company in government sales and military contracts. In addition to working fifty-hour weeks, I was also raising funds for our new church and trying to gain partnerships with other churches, networks, and individual donors. At the time, we had about six thousand dollars in the church bank account and there was an immense amount of pressure to raise financial support. An average week of work in the fall of 2012 was, realistically, about seventy-five hours; forty-five hours at my day job for a paycheck, twenty hours of church-related meetings, and then another ten hours spent raising funds and recruiting partnerships. Most weeks left little time for my wife and kids, who had just uprooted their lives to come on this journey with me. I simply did not have the time to invest in them as much as they needed, and the disconnect was beginning to take its toll.

On January 13, 2013, Awaken Church was born, and we started with a bang. There were 115 people who attended our first service, which was held in an elementary school gymnasium. We launched small groups during the week, and those grew rapidly. Our church was growing in every way possible: dozens of new people each Sunday, rising participation within our small groups, and people giving financially and serving sacrificially. I was watching my vision for this new church come to life, and the excitement was both contagious and motivating. Everyone was celebrating and believed that what we were seeing was truly the miracle we had prayed and hoped for. On the surface, everything looked and felt great, but beneath the surface, there was something simmering that was writing a whole different story.

The core team of people who had moved with us to start this church all worked full-time jobs. While each Sunday brought new faces and excitement, the late nights of work, the weekend planning, and all of the other after-hours logistics made things difficult and exhausting. After adding in my lonely fundraising trips, there were times that this church-planting venture was becoming downright demoralizing to me. It was during one of those trips, sitting in a hotel lobby while watching an NBA game, that I began to believe a dangerous lie:

No one cares as much as me.

As the church took off and increased in success, everyone on our team began celebrating our accomplishments. What they didn't see, and what I failed to communicate, was that our success had created an additional weight of work. As the lead pastor and point leader of this team, I made the decision to carry the majority of the workload by myself because I believed that was what a good leader would do. I put the calls on my to-do list, put the plans on my calendar, and raised all the financial support solo. I was sacrificing an ungodly amount of time away from my wife and kids. I missed zoo trips, beach outings, and movie nights. I recall the late nights of sermon study, the weekends organizing church finances, and the early mornings of compiling small group curriculum. I took on most of these tasks myself because I didn't want to burden my team members, who were either out of town, busy with prior plans, or unable to commit due to existing responsibilities. I began to believe no one cared as much as I did about the success of Awaken Church. I didn't complain. I didn't whine. I refused to quit. I just did what I felt like a good leader should do and got stuff done no matter the cost.

∿

Two months into our church plant, my beautiful wife, Ashley, told me she was pregnant. I'll never forget the night she broke the news as we laid in bed after a typical exhausting day. She seemed reluctant to tell me, but finally got the words out: "Babe, I'm pregnant." The silence that lingered in the room after those words was palpable and painful. Eventually, I just said, "Wow." And not in an excited way. In more of a "my-life-just-got-up-ended-by-a-tornado" kind of way. Then Ashley left the room.

I can still remember staring up at the ceiling fan as it spun rapidly overhead. I compared those fan blades to my life as they were just spinning and spinning and spinning in an effort to try and make something happen. I felt mindless and numb to the news I had just received. Another responsibility. Another expense. Another blessing that seemed like a burden because of the extreme weight of everything else at the time. My perspective was skewed and distorted. The stress of that night and that season was almost too much to bear. Not to mention, Easter was just around the corner.

In the church world, Easter is like the Super Bowl. It's a really big event that everyone looks forward to. It's a time when many people choose to go to church for the first time or go back to church in a search for hope and faith. As a brand-new church coming up on our very first Easter Sunday service, this was a major opportunity we knew we had to capitalize on. We had one desire: to meet and connect with anyone and everyone on that Easter weekend. Our teams were ready, our plans were made, and when the weekend arrived, we had dozens of volunteers prepared to set up chairs and create a welcoming atmosphere for the hundreds of people we would open our doors to the next morning for church. Our momentum was at an all-time high. We were ready to capitalize on all the connections that would come.

One of the faithful volunteers setting up chairs in the recreational center that day was my Ashley. She was working tirelessly alongside several other women in our church to get the room ready for worship services. I was about fifty feet away when I heard several gasps and saw Ashley's face as she began to cry. As I walked towards her, I realized her skin was pale as she looked down at the ground. She was in the midst of a miscarriage. She was embarrassed and visibly upset, even as friends tried to console her. She needed to get home and be checked in to a hospital. Thankfully, we had some amazing friends that day that took her home and gave her the care she needed.

She was humiliated.

She was heartbroken.

She was hurting and so helpless.

Meanwhile ...

I was focused on Easter.

I helped clean the floor right before jumping back into work. I never even left the gym. There was work that had to be done. I stayed for the service and continued setting up the stage and chairs. I felt like I had to. I was convinced no one cared about the church as much as I did. The rows had to be straight. The wires had to be secured. The band couldn't miss a cue and the microphones had to be set up. The signs all needed to be in place and the setting had to be pristine. No one else had as much invested in this as me and **no one else cared as much as me**. I worked late into the evening and believed what I was doing was right and necessary.

That evening, I came home to find Ashley already asleep in our bedroom. I didn't bother to wake her and I didn't even know how to ask how she was feeling. I lay in bed, once again, staring up at the ceiling fan spinning around and around.

As much as it pains me to write this, that day I cared more about a church service than I did about my wife and family. I cared more about work and success than I cared about Ashley's pain and disappointment. I was emotionally detached. I was numb. Looking back, this was one of the darkest moments of my life and ministry. This was one of my worst days as a husband and the day I realized I was losing at what mattered most.

That was the day a lie almost destroyed me.

Passion is a peculiar thing. Depending on the context, it can be a positive attribute or one that ends in total defeat. Every great leader has passion, but what they do with that passion leads to either great success or mass destruction. Passion is what drives leaders to be the best, and it is what others aspire to have as they look on. It is the fire inside our bellies as we give ourselves to the dream and vision of whatever it is we are called to lead. Passion is contagious and infectious, which can be a good thing when used in the right way. However, it can be dangerous if passion turns to pride.

Leaders must realize that passion, if left unchecked, can be poisoned by pride. Pride causes you to elevate yourself over your team. It causes you to question the commitment of others around you. As the one who eats, drinks, and sleeps the vision of your organization, it leads you to believe that others don't do the same. You may see Instagram posts seemingly proving this to be true: others are out on date nights while you're grinding away in your office. They're taking vacations when you haven't had one in over a year. They're clocking in for the minimum number of hours per day while you haven't clocked out since the start. They're eating lunch out and smiling too much and having fun at the expense of your hard work and commitment. You start to believe you're carrying your team, and that belief begins to show physically and emotionally. The added pressure pride creates becomes an unbearable burden. As the leader, you don't complain and you don't whine. You just hustle and grind. Head down. Work harder. Your passion leads you to brandish a badge of honor that embraces the following lie: **no one cares as much as me.** Every day when you wake up, you get dressed and fasten that badge to your chest. All the while, resentment toward those around you is taking root and bitterness builds a wall no one can see but can definitely feel. The wall, the badge, and the root of resentment all point back to pride.

The dangerous part of this lie is how it can lead you into a place of isolation. It can lead you to loneliness and stress as you slowly elevate yourself above your team. When a leader finds themselves in this place, the only person that matters is self and every decision is catered to that preference. Because you believe no one else cares as much as you do, you refuse to trust anyone with anything significant, questioning their motives and their effort. When something goes wrong or a deadline isn't met, the lie causes you to accuse and blame everyone but yourself. Negativity begins to navigate every course of action, and eventually you lose the respect of the people you once locked arms with. As the leader, you end up retracting others' responsibilities, embracing authority, and tightening your grip on the reins of control. You become an all-powerful and overbearing king, convinced that no one cares the way you do. Yet nothing could be further from the truth.

It is important to remember that passion is simply a set of feelings, not facts. The fact is, in most cases, your team actually does care just as much as you do. They have invested blood, sweat, and tears. They think about your passion project after hours, and they lose sleep too. They want to win just as much as you do. If they didn't, they would have left already. Are there times when passion fades? Yes. Are there some people who check out and lose heart? Yes. But that's the exception and not the norm. As a leader, your team is your greatest resource. They are passionate people ready to lock arms with you in whatever fight you are facing. They care about you and your mission. They care about the people you serve and the health of everyone involved. They have chosen to follow you as a leader and they are committed to doing so. The honest truth is this: they care as much as you do. Start loving them, including them, and inviting them into every aspect of the mission. You will become a stronger leader in the process, and you will discover that the weight of your success is much lighter when you share it with those around you.

That Easter, Awaken Church experienced our highest attendance to date, and many of those first-time visitors continued membership with us and are still with us all these years later. We were at the peak of our success as a young church, and while I would love to recall that weekend with fond memories, the one memory that haunts me is the one you just read about. My passion was overcome by pride, which led me to prioritize my work over my wife. The ministry had become my mistress, and I didn't even realize it. I thought I was the only one who cared about the dream being built, and this led to an inflated ego, causing me to work harder and longer than anyone else. My commitment came at the expense of my Ashley, my kids, and my team. You see, when we sow seeds of judgement toward others' assumed lack of passion, we reap the devastation of arrogance and ego. I was blinded by pride and unable to see the enthusiasm and dedication of the team I had in front of me. I knew something had to change if I was going to survive this journey.

In the weeks following that weekend, I chose to reach out to a close friend, who counseled me through the emotions I was feeling. We addressed the emotional disconnect and distance I had been feeling. I was able to process this with Ashley as well. I began to make necessary changes to my schedule and spirit to create a healthy balance between my personal and professional life. I was able to continue building and leading the church while also becoming a more effective husband and leader at home. Eventually, Ashley became pregnant again, and God blessed us with a beautiful daughter, Brooklyn Cate Bowers. She is a constant reminder to me of God's faithfulness. I am grateful now for the journey that allowed me to experience and witness firsthand the danger of passion gone wild. The lesson learned laid a solid foundation for the incredible growth I have experienced since.

Truth #1: Passion is powerful when it's harnessed and humble. When you feel like no one else cares as much as you do, choose to focus on the facts that tell a different story. Passion that becomes prideful limits you

from seeing others' efforts and leads you to isolation. People care just as much as you do; they just might not be as neurotic.

∿

LEADING THROUGH THE LIE

Take a few moments and think about the team you lead. Who doesn't care as much as you do? What has led you to feel that way? Think about the situation or sequence of events that led you to embrace this belief about that person. Have you addressed the problems leading to this point? Have you worked through the conflict or have you chosen to avoid it? Has your passion led you to embrace feelings that have caused you to act in a dangerous or unhealthy way?

As you ponder these questions and think about the people you currently lead, consider taking these steps to overcome the dangerous lie that **no one cares as much as you** and keep your passion in check.

1. *Identify and isolate negative incidents.* Often, it can feel like someone doesn't care because they have failed in some area and left you to pick up the extra work. It might be a missed deadline, an unfinished assignment, or just a lack of availability to help on an after-hours project. While it is unintentional, as the leader, it is easy to compile these incidents into a case file that eventually finds someone "guilty" of

not caring. However, that's simply not true or fair. Take the time to identify each isolated incident rather than combining them into a larger issue.

2. *Address the mess.* This lie creates conflict because its root is pride. Raw feelings raise the temperature of conflict, and even the best leaders choose to avoid these conversations. Rather than calling a meeting to address the issue, they prefer to carry the extra load and quietly deal with the frustration alone. This approach will only push them further away from their team while increasing stress and resentment. The best thing you can do is immediately address the mess, express your emotions, and resolve to work through each conflict as it arises.

3. *Fight your feelings.* One of the greatest gifts you can give your team is your decision to fight against the shifting tides of feelings and anchor yourself to facts. Remember that you have a team committed to your cause. They wake up and come to the office ready to contribute to the vision you have for your company or organization. They are in the battle with you and want to win as well. They are with you and for you even when your feelings tell you otherwise. Choose to lead by facts, not feelings.

CHAPTER 3

MOVE . . . GET OUT OF THE WAY

The way of a fool is right in his own eyes,

but a wise man is he who listens to counsel.

—King Solomon (Proverbs 12:15 NASB)

Lie #2: My way is the best way.

Every leader sits in the seat of leadership for a reason. Skilled musicians, brilliant educators, charismatic speakers, creative innovators, passionate directors of nonprofits, bold pioneers of businesses, successful CEOs, and the list goes on. Every leader has an advanced understanding of their particular field. They are on the cutting edge of trends, practices, and methods to stay ahead of the competition. They want to excel and improve both personally and professionally. Their pursuit of continuous improvement leads to conversations or meetings where problems are identified and solved. These meetings jumpstart discussions and brainstorming. Whether it's three people or thirty people, these meetings are necessary and invaluable to a team's success. However, something dangerous can begin to brew in these settings.

Your strengths and gifts helped you step into the role of leadership. You have positive traits that allow you to solve thousands of problems. You show obvious confidence as you discuss and possibly dominate conversations. Without even realizing it, everyone in the room looks to you as the leader, and you feel a pressure to have an answer, a solution, a way to make things better. With the swirling discussion and the scribbles on the whiteboard, the danger is that, as a leader, you tend to hold the trump card, the ace of spades, the final answer. While the team presents ideas and offers alternative solutions, there is a lie that echoes in the mind of most leaders that sounds something like this ...

My way is the best way.

Three years after starting Awaken Church, I was leading and pastoring the fastest-growing community I had ever been a part of. The pressure and weight of responsibility was unlike anything I had ever experienced before. What began as a small group in my living room just three years prior was now a church of 800 people with multiple worship services, over fifty small groups, and our own church campus. We had just completed a huge building project, requiring added work for myself and my team. Our budget was growing due to the increased generosity of our people, which in turn increased our administrative and fiscal responsibilities. In addition, our staff was growing in number, requiring more development and communication to serve and lead the church. My weekly responsibilities were studying to preach, leading a small group, leading staff development, troubleshooting facility issues, and overseeing our budget while also planning for campus multiplication and coaching other church planters in other cities and states. Additionally, I was married and trying to parent four kids under the age of ten. Did I mention I was drowning?

The pace of leadership during that season was fast. The incredible growth we were experiencing presented daily challenges that needed direct guidance and counsel. There didn't seem to be enough time in the day or week to accomplish the demands around us. It was not unusual for a staff meeting to include the following agenda:

- Prayer & devotion

- Plan Christmas services

- Connect and assimilate twenty-three new families

- Hire an additional staff member

- Create Year-End Financial Report

- Nail down outreach opportunity

- Determine crisis counseling for two married couples

- Develop timeline to launch new church campus

- Solve the global poverty crisis!!

I could tangibly feel such an unhealthy pressure in those moments to simply make decisions. As the leader, I knew everything left undecided would only linger into the following week. Then those unresolved issues would be added to a new set of issues. I knew decisions were necessary, and I had the most experience in the room to be able to make those decisions. With fifteen years of megachurch ministry experience and as the leader who started this church from the ground up, I had the confidence needed for the job, and the staff naturally looked to me as the one who would know the best way. I began to embrace a false reality that my answer was the best answer and that *my way was the best way.* This pattern of problem-solving became permanent, and before I knew it, I was making the majority of the decisions for our team. Ultimately, the process was unhealthy for everyone involved. It fed the problem of pride and handicapped the development of our team. I knew there was a problem and something had to change. I just didn't know how.

I'm assuming you've heard of Moses. Moses is a prominent figure in both Judaism and Christianity. God sent Moses to deliver the Israelites out of bondage and slavery under the evil Egyptian Pharaoh. Moses' life story is recorded in the biblical book of

Exodus and also in the popular movie *The Prince of Egypt*. (I suggest reading the book first and then watching the movie.) Moses was able to lead approximately two million people through a desert toward the promised land of Canaan. His leadership was met with great success, but also with occasional failure.[1]

Moses was the leader and judge for all of the Israelites, and though his work required much of him, he led well. Every day the people would bring cases to Moses for judgement and justice.[2] Just imagine Judge Judy on her bench listening to court cases from 7:30 a.m. until 6:30 p.m. all day every day ... except imagine her with a long, gray beard. Moses would hear cases and render a verdict based on the wisdom and guidance he received from the Lord. You can imagine, with a population of almost two million people who were unaware of how to live as a society of free people, that the court cases were never-ending. The people lined up all day and into the evening with Moses handling all of their cases alone. He was doing the best he could, but it was limiting his time to lead well in other areas. Jethro, Moses' father-in-law, knew the way Moses was doing things would lead to disaster. He had a better idea.

Moses' father-in-law said, "This is no way to go about it. You'll burn out, and the people right along with you. This is way too much for you—you can't do this alone ... You need to keep a sharp eye out for competent men—men who fear God, men of integrity, men who are incorruptible—and appoint them as leaders over groups ... They'll be responsible for the everyday work of judging among the people. They'll bring the hard cases to you, but in the routine cases they'll be the judges. They will share your load and that will make it easier for you. If you handle the work this way, you'll have the strength to carry out whatever God commands you, and the people in their settings will flourish also."[3]

Moses listened to his father-in-law's counsel and followed his advice.[4] It proved to be one of the greatest leadership decisions Moses made. He was able to move forward as a leader and lead the Israelites to Mount Sinai, where he received the Ten Commandments.[5] Without Jethro's godly wisdom and counsel, there's a good chance that Moses would still be stuck in his Judge Judy seat, falling short of everything God intended for him and his people. If we expect to accomplish all that God has laid out for us to do, we must surround ourselves with people who not only see a better way but are willing to speak up and share their ideas for the benefit of the entire organization. **We all need some Jethros in our lives.**

〰️

As the fall of 2016 forged ahead, I was drowning with work and overwhelmed as my team looked to me for almost every decision that needed to be made within our rapidly growing church. In addition to the weekly grind of leading and pastoring a church, I was also trying to stay involved in my kids' lives by coaching their sports teams and being present at home. I was eagerly seeking a healthy work/life balance (which I'm now convinced is somewhat of a myth) and knew a hiring decision needed to be made.

When I finished a personal whiteboard session with my team about what type of skill set I believed we needed to hire, I was disillusioned. We needed a strong, relational leader; a financial genius; an expert in budgeting and building; a keeper of staff culture; and someone with a calling to full-time, vocational ministry. And I needed to actually like them, because that matters too. Basically, I needed a unicorn. A person who encompasses all of those qualities is a rare breed in the world of church ministry. However, it was what we needed. I prayed hard and specifically that God would bring us ... well, a unicorn. A Jethro, if you will.

I'll never forget the day Shawn Ferguson asked me to grab some coffee to discuss his life, his career, and his newfound calling. Shawn was a very faithful member of our church and was also a rising star in the world of professional soccer. Playing locally with the Charleston Battery Soccer Club of the United Soccer League, Shawn was named the club's Captain and also recognized on the First Team All-USL Team. At the close of the 2015 season, he found himself at a true crossroads both personally and professionally. While there were opportunities to continue playing soccer professionally, there was also a desire to pursue ministry and join our staff and utilize many of the same leadership qualities to shape our staff and culture as a team. Shawn knew the needs that existed on our staff; his incredible wife Karlee was already serving full-time as our Communications Director. They were a power couple in every sense of the term, and they were both excelling in their respective careers. I knew this meeting with Shawn would have monumental implications for their family and his sports career. However, I could have never known just how important and instrumental this meeting would prove to be for the future and advancement of our church.

That was the day God brought me a unicorn.

Shawn retired from soccer and came on staff a few months later. He began overseeing all of our financial processes while also leading the vision and strategic direction of our church ministries. He quickly became my Jethro. He proved to be a great decision-maker, but more importantly, he empowered the team under him to do the same. His wisdom and insight on how to filter information and delegate decision-making was a game changer within our organization, allowing us to fly farther with more ownership than I ever could have imagined.

Shawn proved to be one of the sharpest leaders I have ever known, and I still find myself regularly looking to him when challenges and obstacles arise. The truth is, his ways are often much better than mine. Together, we have built a team that brings vision and sound strategy into every meeting as decisions and plans are made. I am no longer always seen as the "smartest person in the room," which is one of the greatest compliments to our team. We are much better together and much stronger as a whole. While it has been a humbling process for me as a leader, it has also been one of the most liberating adventures of my life. There is freedom in knowing that not every decision depends on you. And trust me on this: as a leader, I can promise you that **your way is not always the best way.**

When pride poisons passion, it can often lead to thoughts of "my way or the highway." Confidence is an absolute necessity as a leader, but when it morphs into pride, it can limit your team and leave you burnt out. By having Jethros in our lives, we can keep our confidence in check, make sure everyone's voices are heard, and see that the best practices are implemented. Allow your team to be autonomous and creative; that's when amazing things happen.

> **Truth #2: A necessary partner to confidence is counsel. Confidence turned prideful leads to ineffectiveness. Figure out where you need to get out of the way so that your team's innovation and creativity can thrive.**

LEADING THROUGH THE LIE

Think about the atmosphere of your meetings and discussions. Are you providing the most solutions for your team? Do you feel an unnecessary amount of pressure to be right? Does every decision stop on your desk? Are you good at receiving feedback and accepting alternative ideas? Do you believe your way is always the best way? Consider implementing the following principles in order to overcome and lead through the lie that **"my way is the best way"** and ensure that your confidence is tempered with humility.

1. *Choose to share last.* When a topic is on the table for discussion, make it a discipline to listen to your team's ideas first. As the leader, it is typical for your team to withhold ideas out of respect for the one you put on the table. This can unfortunately cause the best "ways" to never be voiced. Choose to share last and see what surfaces.

2. *Ask for help.* When you feel the pressure to always provide an answer or the "best way," ask for help. Give your team permission to push back. Trust the team you have been given. When you don't know, say so. Be humble enough to ask for help. This will allow your team to flourish rather than fail.

3. *Change the room.* If it seems like you are the most experienced and most knowledgeable person in the room, figure out a way to change the room. This does not necessarily mean hiring a new team. It may simply mean stepping out of the room. Who's at the meetings? What meetings do you need to step out of? You will be amazed at the solutions that surface when you are out of the room. Trust your team. Watch what happens. Also, consider who you can

meet with outside the organization to offer more objective guidance. How can you get in a room with people who know better than you? How can you hear from voices that can offer new ways of doing things? In summary, think about the voices influencing the team. If your voice is always the best voice offering the best way, it is time to shift the strategy.

CHAPTER 4

CULTURE IS THE MAIN COURSE

Culture eats strategy for breakfast.

—Peter Drucker[1]

Lie #3: Culture is overrated.

The greatest chicken sandwich in the world is made by Chick-Fil-A. It's true. Hands down. Don't even try to argue it. Last year, they sold more than 290 million chicken sandwiches to people just like you and me. However, that figure pales in comparison to the 3 billion chicken sandwiches they've sold since opening their doors in 1967. The same sandwich made the same way and sold by the same restaurant. Fascinating, isn't it? The Chick-Fil-A chicken sandwich has been setting records since before we put a man on the moon. Take a moment and just list out all the things that have changed and adapted in our culture since the 1960s.

Hairstyles. Fashion trends. Musical genres and groups. Artistic expressions. The TV shows that have come and gone. The retail stores that have launched and been lost. The restaurants you once loved that are now a distant memory. The fads and trends that once flourished and have now faded. So much has changed. Yet, the Chick-Fil-A chicken sandwich remains. And not just remains—it has enjoyed a fifty-year climb to the top. Know why?

Culture.

In 1961, a young entrepreneur by the name of Truett Cathy came across a discovery that would shift the course of human history: a pressure cooker that could fry a chicken patty in the same amount of time it took to cook a fast-food hamburger. This was a game changer because up until that moment, it simply was not feasible to create quality chicken sandwiches at a pace fit to serve the fast-food customer. Truett Cathy discovered a diamond in the fast-food business, and he knew it. He began paving the pathway for Chick-Fil-A.

In 1967, after spending several years perfecting his recipe and the process to create it, Cathy opened the very first Chick-Fil-A in a shopping mall. Truett made the purpose of Chick-Fil-A clear to all employees: "We should be about more than just selling chicken. We should be a part of our customers' lives and the communities in which we serve."[2] With his signature slogan across all operations, "We Didn't Invent the Chicken, Just the Chicken Sandwich," Cathy began to sell thousands of sandwiches and opened many different locations. As of 2018, Chick-Fil-A is still owned by the Cathy family and boasts over 2,200 stores raking in over $8 billion in revenue, all while being a *private, Christian* company that is *closed on Sundays.*

What I love about Chick-Fil-A is how their culture is consistent and their purpose hasn't changed. The statement of purpose at Chick-Fil-A is "To glorify God by being a faithful steward of all that is entrusted to us and to have a positive influence on all who come into contact with Chick-Fil-A." That is a strong, clear purpose. They have become a force to be reckoned with because of the quality of their food and the culture they've built. It's become a brand identity that has set them apart in the world of fast-food restaurants. While most Christian companies struggle to integrate into mainstream society, Chick-Fil-A has not only integrated but has become the prominent leader of their industry. They're even celebrated and promoted by mainstream media; just check out the song "Closed on Sunday" by Kanye West! It really is fascinating how a clear purpose and culture will set the course of your company … and your life.

There's a popular story about Truett Cathy that speaks volumes about the strength and clarity of Chick-Fil-A's culture. One day at Chick-Fil-A's corporate headquarters, a meeting was called to discuss issues at hand and determine the best path forward for the company. While the room was buzzing with ideas, down at the end of the table sat Truett Cathy in complete silence. For hours, the discussion centered around how to grow bigger and faster in order to keep their competitive edge until, the meeting ended abruptly when Cathy slammed his fist on the table and said, "Gentlemen, I am sick and tired of hearing you talk about us getting bigger! If we get better, then our customers will demand we get bigger."[3]

The meeting was over.

Culture had spoken.

ʍ

Culture is the most important component of any organization. It is the shared attitudes, values, goals, and practices of the team or business. It is the language used, the statements quoted, and the stories shared and celebrated. A strong culture supports the vision and mission of the organization. A weak culture doesn't even know what that means. A strong culture provides clear values and expectations for all members of the team. A weak culture has vague values, which creates insecure members due to the lack of stated expectation. A strong culture upholds the steady voice of its leader and follows that leader's voice in the pursuit of success. A weak culture gives the leader an unstable voice that is unsure where success is to be found.

The emphasis on culture is a relatively new phenomenon in the world of leadership and business development. Though its impact on performance and progress in the workplace has been known for some time, the concept of culture has often been misunderstood due in large part to the ambiguity of its meaning and definition. It is not uncommon for some leaders to believe the lie that **culture is overrated**. While culture is being talked and written about more than ever, that does not mean it is a fad or trend that will fade away. Culture is here to stay, and if you plan to be a great leader, it is time you embrace the need to create a strong and defined culture in the area in which you lead.

While it can seem like an intangible or vague concept, the reality is quite the opposite. To be a great leader, you must begin to embrace culture as a driver and a catalyst to propel your team to greater success. It is the incubator in which your strategy for growth and brand enhancement will be nurtured and developed. It is the atmosphere and environment that encompasses everyone you lead. It is the framework that surrounds everything you do, and by defining it clearly, it will chart the course of what health and success will look like for you as a leader. Not only will you benefit personally from the clarity of your culture, your team will also recognize the advantages and credit you with being brave and bold enough to define the details of who you actually are as an organization. Culture is, by all means, the element that will either make you or break you.

It took me almost three years to realize how important culture was in the church that I was leading. We were a young church, scaling rapidly as we grew to almost a thousand people in attendance and a staff of a dozen people. The leadership challenges that accompany this type of growth are numerous: systems management, volunteer empowerment, financial processes, communications, graphic design, worship and production, staff development, leadership training, and also care and counseling, just to name a few. Each of these areas had to be properly developed while maintaining continuous growth every weekend. Looking back, it seems as though every time we figured out how to manage a certain process, that process required immediate adaptation and change to embrace the growth we experienced.

As the leader of our team, I was not allocating enough time to properly onboard people to our staff. Even if I had, there was not a defined culture to be taught and caught within our staff. The key word is "defined" because, while we didn't have it on paper, we definitely had a culture. Every organization and team does. There was an abundance of ambiguity and mountains of stress, and some days I know several of my faithful team members dreamed of having jobs where they felt more valued and included in the goals and direction of the organization. There was tension on our team, and I was having a hard time determining the reason why. Even though we were winning on the outside, we felt a sense of loss because the joy in doing our jobs was diminishing. I knew just enough about leadership to realize that these were unhealthy emotions and fluctuations, especially while we were experiencing exponential growth. This prompted me to make a phone call that would change everything.

Richie Shaw pastors Real Life Ministries in Spokane, Washington, a large church also experiencing tremendous growth and success. He had coached me in the early years of launching the church, so I knew he would be able to speak into my blind spots and understand some of my struggles. Our conversation the following day proved to be one of the most pivotal for my life and ministry.

I opened our conversation by explaining the obstacles and staff issues I was dealing with. To be honest, I was secretly hoping he would just tell me to resign and come work for him. I explained all the dynamics and tensions I was facing and how, even though we were accelerating in terms of growth and success, there were still feelings of failure and loss. It took him about two seconds to diagnose my issue. He said, "Brandon, here's the deal. You've gotta define the values of your culture."

He went on to explain how everyone has a set of intrinsic values they operate in connected to their core purpose, and that shapes the way they see and do things. I was leading out of an assumption that everyone operated with the same personal values and culture as me.

The same heart.

The same work ethic.

The same hustle.

The same grit.

The same passion.

The same eye for excellence.

All of that.

However, this was not true. He explained that while I may wish and even want everyone to have this set of values and operate the same way, it simply wasn't going to happen. The disconnect and tensions we were experiencing were anchored in this issue of culture, stemming from the fact that we were misaligned as a team in *how* we wanted to get things done. I had a purpose fueling my work and helping me to accomplish my dream, but pride infiltrated my purpose and led to cultural blind spots and disunity. A light bulb came on for me, and I set out on a mission to define the culture of Awaken Church for my team.

Richie suggested starting by grabbing a journal and writing out my own set of personal values as they pertain to culture. As the leader, you will naturally lead out of who you are. The sooner you can identify those traits, the better. I slotted a full day on my calendar and spent it at the beach, just me and a chair and a journal. I spent time evaluating who I was and what I truly valued as a person and a leader. I began to write statements such as "I risk the ocean," revealing the way I value making decisions based on faith instead of fear. Another statement read, "Our invitation deserves excellence," revealing my belief that anything I do in the name of Jesus deserves my absolute best in every aspect possible.

In my beach chair, I reflected on all my years of leading and of serving under great leaders. I had never truly evaluated before why I thought, felt, and acted the way I did. Between the seagulls, the occasional ocean swimming, and the sunburns, I was able to compile ten phrases that defined my personal culture as a leader and fully explained the "how" by which I choose to live and lead. I left the beach motivated to share my personal "culture code," as I called it, with my staff in an effort to define who we were going to be as a cohesive unit moving forward together. It was apparent that, while I truly appreciated everyone on my team at Awaken Church, we could not move forward without creating consistency with a cultural standard.

So we went to Boot Camp.

That's right—we hosted a two-day Culture Boot Camp for our staff and key leaders. We spent our time reviewing stories from our history that we felt defined us as a team. Stories shape culture. They become what you celebrate and desire to replicate. Stories of innovation with limited resources or saying "no" to good things because they were competing with the best things on our calendar. Stories of people who rose through our leadership pipeline to make a major difference within our church. These stories revealed many values that we, as a team, felt were integral pieces to who we were as an organization.

In addition to sharing and processing stories, we had everyone carry out the same practice of listing out their personal intrinsic values that shaped who they were as a person. Then we compiled and compared those lists, and what began to evolve was a collaboration of culture that began to define our organization and team. We started to see that, although certain phrases were worded differently, the underlying principles of what we were saying seemed shockingly similar. Our staff and leadership had consistent DNA, and this was a beautiful thing. We had much more in common than I would have originally guessed. While there were definitely some outliers, there was overwhelming consistency.

We took these individual lists and began to combine and paraphrase them into ten key phrases. We named this the Culture Code of Awaken Church. This code defines how we live, work, and play on our ministry team. Each point on our code is followed by a brief summary of its meaning, and each point of the Culture Code holds stories of origin that outline its history and illustrate its principles. The Culture Code has provided us a blueprint for the identity of our team and, as an overflow, the leadership and life of our entire church. The culture of Awaken Church reflects our mission to love God and represent Him on this earth. Our culture code is defined as follows:

CULTURE CODE of AWAKEN CHURCH

WE'RE A JESUS-LED MOVEMENT.

We are called to carry out a movement
that Jesus already started.
It all starts with Him and it is all because of Him.

WE EMBRACE CHANGE.

Healthy things grow and growing things change.
We embrace change as we continue to grow and get better.

WE RISK THE OCEAN.

We believe that faith acts first and asks later. We will take risks as deep and as wide as the ocean. The same God who created the ocean will always carry us.

WE LOVE LEADERSHIP.

Time is too short to manage people or programs. We are committed to developing leaders who will change the world.

OUR INVITATION DESERVES EXCELLENCE.

Everything we do has eternal implications. Therefore, we will lead with passion, drive, and excellence in all things.

HONOR IS OUR ATTITUDE.

We will honor, at all times, in word and deed, those who lead us, those we serve, and those we serve alongside.

WE DO MORE BY DOING LESS.

We believe simplicity is the trademark of genius. We are committed to being a simple church with streamlined ministry. We have said yes to the best and we will say no to the rest.

WE GO AFTER THE ONE.

We will leave the ninety-nine every time and go after the one. We are more interested in reaching those who are lost than retaining those who are found.

WE'LL BE KNOWN FOR WHAT WE'RE FOR.

We want to be known for what we're for, not against.

We will use our words to speak life

and hope into a world desperate to hear it.

WE'RE IN IT TO WIN IT.

We're out to win the race that's been assigned to us.

We won't settle for the second-best version of our mission.

We will focus through failure and always strive to get better.

We framed posters of our Culture Code and hung them all throughout our offices. The posters were placed everywhere and anywhere that major decisions are made. Our team put it up on our website where people checking out our church online could see it so they would know exactly what they would be stepping into. As lead pastor, I wrote individual blog posts about each piece of our culture code and then taught our key leadership about it as well. We made shirts and did about everything possible to raise awareness of our clearly defined culture. Even today, the Culture Code is the litmus test for new staff as they onboard to our team, and we still point team members back to our code in reminding them to hold to the standards of the culture we aspire to.

Defining our culture has created a powerful and visible alignment. We are now able to provide clarity to our purpose in seasons when questions arise. And while we don't always act according to what we say we value, we are able to gently remind each other of who we desire to be. Finally, we found the alignment and unity we were looking for, both on our staff and among our leadership. Now, when decisions need to be made or difficulties arise, our culture determines our course of action and serves as a compass of decision-making for our entire organization.

Whether you are an entrepreneur launching a new business or the CEO of an entire organization, you have personal values that define you as a person. Things that make you jump out of bed in the morning. Things that inspire and motivate you. Things that make you tick and keep you up at night. And guess what? So does everyone else around you. Most people coast through life without ever doing the hard work of figuring out who they are and what their values are. Even though what we do directly reflects who we are, people rarely make the connection to culture. Many leaders undermine the value of creating culture, yet find themselves frustrated with the very culture they've created.

Let me encourage you to do the hard work of reflecting on and determining who you are as leader and what values you carry. Take the time to process this. It will not only help you to become a better leader but it will directly benefit every interpersonal relationship in your life. You will be a better spouse, parent, friend, and coworker. You will begin to see your life through a different lens that will provide clarity in conversations and decisions. You will begin to appreciate your contribution to culture while gaining a desire to help shape the existing culture around you. Then, as you lead yourself into this awareness, you can begin to lead those around you to do the same. You will begin to bring about change in the world rather than simply existing in the world. You will begin to shift the world around you and make the positive impact you desire on those around you. Your work will be more profitable, your team will be more engaged and appreciative, and you will begin to see the outcomes of creating the culture you truly desire to live and work within. I mean, you're a builder and a creator, right? So get to work and start changing the world.

> **Truth #3: When you know your purpose, your culture will follow. Purpose turned prideful leads to blind spots and disunity. When your purpose is clear and your culture reflects your purpose, you will have clarity and unity.**

$$\sim\!\!\wedge\!\!\wedge$$

LEADING THROUGH THE LIE

As you reflect on the attitudes, values, and practices of the people you lead, do you like what you see and feel? Does everyone operate with the same passion and fervor as you? Are there certain behaviors that irritate you, or perhaps behaviors that inspire you? Are there certain people who have the "it" factor while others just don't seem to get it at all? As the leader, it is important for you to think through the reason why these differing answers exist and what you can do to get everyone on the same page.

Consider the following steps to help define your culture and align your team behind it.

1. *State your personal values first.* Culture flows from the top in every organization. As the leader, you will always have certain intrinsic values that matter to you and must be respected by those you lead. It cannot be manufactured or manipulated. Who you are will eventually come out. Get away and get some time to yourself. Make a list of the values that are meaningful to you and will be present as you lead.

2. *Take an assessment of the current culture.* Teach your team the value of culture and explain what it means. Then have everyone list out ten phrases that define the strengths of your team (e.g. innovative, excited, fun) and five phrases that define the weaknesses of your team (e.g. hasty decisions, reactive rather than proactive). Once everyone on the team contributes to these lists, compile them into one comprehensive list. This will be your current culture definition. Review the lists and determine commonalities. Condense the culture into cohesive statements embodying the feedback from your team. This is your current culture.

3. *Define your ideal culture.* As the leader, you get to define the culture and create the vision to embrace

it. This is a key step in shifting culture as an organization. While there will be aspects of your current assessment that need to be eliminated, it is important to create a culture that is both ideal and attainable. Do this with the top leaders in your organization, such as a board or executive staff. While the entire team does not need to create this, it is important to note that their feedback and assessment will help shape it.

4. ***Declare it and display it.*** Once you define your culture, it is time to declare it. Start with your top leadership and ensure they will own it. Then introduce it to the rest of your team. Teach it and train it so it will be as effective as possible. I cannot overstate the importance of this step. A defined culture is meaningless if the definitions are not understood and embraced. Make your own posters. Put it on your website. Do whatever is necessary to get people to see it, believe it, and bleed it. Everyone will benefit in the process.

CHAPTER 5

PROGRESS, NOT PERFECTION

I've missed more than 9,000 shots in my career. I've lost almost 300 games. Twenty-six times I've been trusted to take the game winning shot and missed. I've failed over and over and over again in my life. And that is why I succeed.

—Michael Jordan[1]

Lie #4: Failure is final.

I am continually fascinated by how real the stories of the Bible are. I know the Bible is regarded as "the Good Book," "the Word," and "the Holy Scriptures," but if you take a step back and contextualize the content, the Bible is a collection of real stories about real people who are more like you than you may think. The characters are real people. Husbands. Wives. Dads and moms. Friends and foes. They lived in big cities and small towns and in many places that still exist today. When I read the Bible, I do everything I can to put myself into the stories and personalize the accounts. I've found that practicing this exercise while reading the Bible not only makes it much easier to understand but also makes it come to life.

One of the characters in the Bible I consistently identify with is Peter. Peter was one of Jesus' disciples and, in my humble opinion, the most intriguing. While it may fly in the face of your church's stained-glass window, Peter was no saint. Peter was rough around the edges. He was a fisherman who got up early and worked until late at night. He fought for his fishing spot each day on the shores of the Sea of Galilee. He was blue-collar and worked hard to make a living. He was not some passive altar boy, desperate to be close to God. No, I'm convinced Peter accepted Jesus' invitation to follow Him because he was tired. He was exhausted. He was looking for something more, even though he couldn't verbalize it. He was looking for a new way of life.

The stories written about Peter are truly fascinating. He was there when Jesus restored sight to the blind. He was there when Jesus multiplied fish and bread to feed thousands. Peter helped pass out the food and collect the leftovers. Peter was there when Jesus calmed a raging storm, and he was there when Jesus walked on water. And Peter walked on water too. In fact, they are the only two people in history who have ever done that! Peter had a front-row seat to three years of Jesus' life and ministry. However, one of Peter's most well-known stories is a story of his failure.

During the Last Supper in the book of John, Jesus and His disciples had dinner together before His death. Jesus told His disciples that one of them would deny Him three times before a rooster crowed.[2] Peter deflected the accusation, "Oh, he's definitely not talking about me. He's talking about one of you guys!" Shortly after that conversation, Jesus was arrested and all the disciples scattered in fear of being arrested themselves by the Roman soldiers. Peter then found himself sitting alone near a campfire next to a group of people he didn't know. A teenage girl quickly spotted him and told everybody he was a friend and follower of Jesus. Knowing the implications of being identified as such, Peter quickly dismissed the idea and told the girl she didn't know what she was talking about. However, she was persistent, as teenagers are, and became even louder in her announcement that he was most definitely a friend and disciple of Jesus. Peter, as politely as possible, told her to shut up as he tried to maintain his cover and avoid being arrested as well. He was trying his best to just blend in with the crowd and let the chaos of the night calm down. Then, after the same girl puts Peter on blast for a third time, he yells back in denial saying he doesn't even know a man named Jesus! Then, the rooster let out a loud crow. The very thing Jesus said would happen, did. Peter was now in the midst of his nightmare. He had denied Jesus and failed as both a friend and follower.[3]

When Peter realized his mistake, he began to weep. This wasn't the kind of failure that you quickly move past, like when he doubted Jesus' ability to multiply bread or when he attempted to keep children away from Jesus. No, this failure was different. It felt permanent and had major consequences. This was a big deal. And he started to believe the lie:

Failure is final.

Peter believed that his lapse in loyalty leading to a failure of faith is what he would be marked for and remembered by. But his story didn't end there. After Jesus was crucified, buried and resurrected, one of the first people he came looking for was Peter. He came to Peter and encouraged him, forgave him, and ultimately, redeemed him.[4] We must remember that before Jesus was crucified, He gave Peter a new name which carried with it a calling, "I say to you that you are Peter, and upon this rock I will build My church."[5] Peter's calling didn't change just because he had failed. Jesus was quick to remind him of this when He forgave him in a conversation over breakfast on the beach. And one of the most beautiful aspects of this conversation is that the other disciples heard it take place. It's as if Jesus wanted all of them to know that just because Peter has made a mistake and failed in his faith, that failure was not fatal. Peter still had a hope and a future because he had a relationship with Jesus. We would all do well to remember that same truth. However, there was one disciple who wasn't at this breakfast and didn't hear this truth: Judas.

Judas was another disciple who also betrayed Jesus on that same night. He was the one who made it possible for Jesus to be arrested when he sold him out to the Roman soldiers for thirty pieces of silver, or about three hundred dollars. When Judas realized the impact of his decision, the guilt was too much to bear and he ended up taking his own life.[6] He succumbed to the lie that his failure was final and that there was no chance for redemption. That lie, unfortunately, took Judas all the way to the grave.

Peter is honored and revered by Christians as the most relatable saint. People can connect with his shortcomings and aspire to have his level of impact. But this is not true for Judas. No one looks up to Judas, even though they both betrayed Jesus that night. Why? What's the difference? Perspective: the ability to acknowledge a mistake yet continue on mission. The ability to fail while still moving forward. Though Peter's passion for Jesus was temporarily poisoned by pride and self-preservation, he ultimately overcame the lie and changed the world. Peter accepted Jesus' words as truth, and that truth shaped his perspective as he moved forward to become one of the most prominent preachers of the gospel. Peter planted and pastored the first church that multiplied into the billions of believers that there are today. He never denied Jesus again, even when it meant his own death. Peter had passion and proper perspective, and that made him an incredible leader who changed the world.

Everybody fails in this life. It's inevitable. It's part of living. Everybody goes through it. Have you ever seen a toddler try to walk? How many attempts did it take for you to ride a bike?

Did you ever strike out or miss a basketball shot? How did you do on your first driving test? Did every girl or guy you asked out on a date say yes? Did you get into every college you applied to? Have you ever gotten a speeding ticket? Or started a diet? Or been declined for a job? You get the point.

We all had to learn how to walk. We learned to ride a bike. We finally made the sports team. We got a driver's license. And yes, we may have gotten scraped up along the way, but eventually we made it happen. Throughout life, we failed repeatedly on our way to eventual success. Along the way, we somehow managed to pull ourselves up by our bootstraps and keep going. We took the next test, removed the training wheels, and practiced as much as it took. We made it.

Now let me ask you a question. Could you imagine for a moment what would have happened if these failures along the way had sidelined us? What if we just gave up when things got hard? Just threw in the proverbial towel and tucked our chins? Game over. You know what? We'd all still be crawling, uneducated, and still sitting in disappointment. It would be a sad, sad story. And in some cases, it is. But for the most part, people like you and me overcome failure every day and experience success on a regular basis.

Some people bounce back from failure in the most incredible ways. Some of the greatest leaders, athletes, businessmen, and politicians have risen to phenomenal success in the wake of failures that should have ended them.

Michael Jordan didn't make the varsity basketball team his sophomore year of high school.

Oprah Winfrey was fired from her first job after being told she was unfit for TV.

Winston Churchill failed the sixth grade.

Jay-Z was unable to get a record deal for his first album.

Henry Ford went bankrupt. Twice.

J. K. Rowling watched *Harry Potter and the Philosopher's Stone* get rejected by all twelve major publishers.

Thomas Edison's teachers told him he was too stupid to learn anything.

Walt Disney had a newspaper boss tell him "he had no imagination or good ideas."

Abraham Lincoln was a failed businessman.

Jerry Seinfeld was booed off the stage at his first stand-up gig.[7]

Can you imagine a world without Jay-Z, Disney movies, Mustangs, or Jordans? Me neither. Yet that would be our reality if it weren't for the incredible decisions that these individuals made to overcome failure and move forward in the face of it. And for each of these failures we know about, there are thousands more that we will never see.

It is one thing to fail as an individual and bounce back, but it can seem even more intimidating when you are a leader and many people look to you and depend on you. When you are the leader trying to lead your team to success, how do you face and fight failure when so many people will be directly affected by the outcome? I believe it is the leader's attitude toward failure that changes everything. Are you resilient in the face of failure? Or are you easily sidelined by it?

Most people will never see the difficulties that shape a leader from day to day. They won't see the declined grant proposal, the unreturned phone calls, the blistering emails, the people who walk away, the profit/loss sheets, the rejected ideas, or the emotions from a meeting that went south. But you will. And if you lead long enough, you will discover that those small failures from the day-to-day grind have the power to do you in if you let them. I call those failures paper cuts. Individually, none of them will be fatal, but collectively they can lead to massive loss and deep scars. You must learn how to face these struggles head-on and determine to push through failure when it happens. Your ability to lead through failure will determine your success. It's hard. It's messy. But it is absolutely necessary if you are going to make it as a leader.

I learned that the hard way.

In the spring of 2015, the church I started was only two years old. We had grown to about 350 people, and we were renting a traditional Baptist church building in a suburban area of our city.

The building was old and dilapidated. The carpet was shot, the wood pews were faded, there were missing window panes, and there was no working air conditioning. The church had gone on for years without any improvements or renovations, and to say it was in bad shape would have been an understatement. We rented that building because we needed a place to hold church services and they needed the funds. They were a dying congregation with bills that needed to be paid. We were a growing congregation that needed the space. In an ideal world, we could have just merged together and become one church. However, this was no ideal situation. Not by any stretch of the imagination.

We had our worship service at 9:00 a.m. and we filled the place. It was beautiful. The sanctuary was filled and the overflow filled a balcony that hadn't seen use in several decades. The kids' rooms were filled to the door, and the volume was noticeable. There weren't even enough parking spaces, so people parked on the grass and the side streets. We were filled to the last chair and it felt amazing, but there was a problem. We had to be completely out by 10:40 a.m.

By out, I mean *out*. Gone. Every person, every kid, every car, every sign, and everything representing Awaken Church had to leave the premises. That meant moving hundreds of people physically off the property in less than twenty minutes after the service ended. And not only that, everything had to be put back in the proper place and in perfect condition as requested by the church we rented from. While it seems absurd, this was the only way we could continue renting the space. As you can imagine, this was a massive effort from volunteers that understood we were desperate to use the facility. There was a weekly struggle of trying to maintain a good rental relationship so the church I was leading would not only survive but also thrive. Here was our problem: our city prohibited us from using any of the schools, and we were priced out by the commercial leasing market (Charleston was and still is one of the top real estate markets in the country). The bottom line was this: it was necessary to delicately manage this rocky relationship so our young church could have a home. Even if it was just a rental.

Well, in the spring of 2015, I blew it.

We were at capacity. We had no air conditioning. I couldn't care less where people parked. The disgruntled neighbors around the church quieted down after we walked around and handed out gift cards. The real problems were the lack of air conditioning during summer heat reaching over ninety degrees and 100 percent humidity and the overflowing kids' space. I knew that we couldn't continue to grow unless we made more room, so the next logical thing to try was an additional worship service to hopefully regulate the congestion of people. We could add the new service either after lunch or in the evening.

My team went to a meeting where we requested to add another service, purchase the church property, or allow the renters to donate the property through a partnership, if they were willing to allow our congregations to join together as one. I thought the meeting went well and that we talked through each possibility in detail.

I left that meeting and boarded a plane to Dallas, Texas to attend a men's conference at Prestonwood Church where thousands of men would come together for worship, inspiration, and encouragement in their faith. Led by Pastor Jack Graham, Prestonwood is one of the most influential churches in America. And because we were a sponsored church plant in the Prestonwood Network, I was excited to be going there with great news of our growth and the tremendous success we were experiencing. I felt the timing was right to get away, get inspired, and get reenergized for Easter, which was only two weeks away. I can still remember being on that plane with big dreams! I truly believed that when I returned, Awaken Church would be able to add another service, possibly purchase the church property, and continue to see the growth of our church take place. Little did I know what was about to happen.

We got kicked out.

I still have the letter.

It was Palm Sunday when I got back from Dallas. I showed up to preach that morning and there was a letter in my office mailbox. It stated in very clear terms that the church that held the rights to the building was no longer interested in continuing their rental agreement with us. We were told to begin looking for another place and to keep them informed of our progress in doing so. I can still feel the weight on my chest as I read those words that morning. I could not believe it. I folded up the letter, walked downstairs, and preached my heart out in front of a packed house for Palm Sunday. I sang. I prayed. I preached. I shook hands and kissed babies. And then I got in my car and cried.

I had failed miserably.

I had just sealed the fate of our church.

I had ruined the relationship with our rental.

I had just driven our church to homelessness.

I had no idea what to do next.

I stayed up that night and read my Bible. I would like to say that I always do that when times get hard, but that'd be a lie. But on this night, I was reading my Bible and reviewing the notes I had jotted down at the conference I had just attended. The notes were about risk-taking because we serve a trustworthy God who is in control of all things. It was there in those notes that I found hope. I was reminded that God would make a way; He would enable and empower me to lead our church in this season of uncertainty. In that moment of hope, I remembered meeting a guy named Scott Olson while I was in Dallas. Scott was a faithful member of Prestonwood and a major supporter of the Prestonwood Network. When I met Scott, I learned that he loved Charleston and vacationed to Kiawah Island each year with his family. He had heard about what God was doing through our church and said that if he could ever help to let him know. I also learned that he was involved in commercial real estate. While I didn't know Scott that well, I knew that I now needed him. So I decided to pick up the phone and capitalize on his offer to help. And it was the call that changed everything.

I called Scott on Monday morning and told him about the letter. I told him about how my original plan had failed and how we needed to come up with a new one, and fast. He asked about our demographics, our financial situation, and what flexibility we might have with potential locations. We covered a lot of ground in terms of details and numbers and specifics, but what made the biggest impact on me about that initial conversation with Scott boils down to this: his faith. I will forever remember explaining our situation to him and waiting for some kind of rebuke. I had so many assumptions about what he would say in response to my failure through the phone call, but what came out of his mouth struck me like few words ever have.

"Brandon, this isn't the end. You know that, right? God's got this, and we're going to figure it out together."

With his encouragement and perspective, I knew Awaken Church would bounce back. We were resilient. We'd get through this. **This failure was not final.**

We went on to find a new location and embark on a massive building project that grew our faith as a church beyond what we could have imagined. I watched the people of our congregation rally behind the vision and make tremendous sacrifices, allowing us to move into a permanent church building that has seen thousands of people walk through its doors. I have witnessed what can happen when a leader overcomes initial failure and finds the strength to forge ahead against all odds. I have also realized there are times when boldness must be borrowed from people like Scott Olson. I have vowed to be that person for other people when it's needed, and my prayer is that you would agree to be the same. As a leader and pastor, I find it a joy to offer hope and encouragement when others come to me with their own challenges and failures. It is so important to believe in the truth that failure is not final and help others to see and believe that, as well.

The question is not *if* we will fail, but how we'll respond when we do. Failure is inevitable, but it is not final. When we let pride and self-pity lead us to think we are beyond redemption, we begin to believe the lie that has the power to immobilize us. When we choose to stand back up after being knocked down and learn from our failures, we become better leaders. There's no such thing as a perfect leader—the sooner you get comfortable with that, the more successful you will be. Like Peter, you don't have to be faultless in order to make a huge, positive impact in this world. You just have to be willing to stand back up and keep walking forward.

Truth #4: With proper perspective, losses become lessons. Your ability to get back up after failure will ensure that it is not final. Passion turned prideful leads to self-pity whenever we fail. Perspective is what helps us get back up, dust ourselves off, and keep moving forward.

〰

LEADING THROUGH THE LIE

Everyone handles failure differently. It is important to understand what your tendencies are and how you respond. Your leadership and the way you handle failure will determine by example how others on your team will see and respond to failure. You have the power to personally shape the attitude toward failure within your team or organization. As you reflect on what this means for you moving forward, let me offer three pieces of advice that have helped me manage failure in both my own life and in the lives of those I lead.

1. ***Don't make it personal.*** "I failed" is very different from "I'm a failure." Learn the difference. You are not what you do. This is by far the most difficult dynamic to overcome. Don't let your identity get hijacked by your position. Make the decision to place your value and worth in something greater than your failures or successes. For me, this is where faith has been my saving grace. Take time to discover what that means for you.

2. ***Learn and let it go.*** I have no problem making a mistake. I have a problem making the same mistake twice. Failure is a great teacher. Be a student. Learn from it. It is important, as a leader, that you learn from letdowns and allow them to make you better. When failure happens, take notes. Write them down. Journal it. Share what you learned with your team.

Everyone will benefit from the lesson. And then let it go. Move on. Don't dwell on it. One of the greatest things you can do is forgive yourself. You can't move forward if you're focused on what's behind. Learn and let it go.

3. ***Don't worry about what others think.*** More often than not, our fear of failure is rooted in what other people think. Stop giving so much power away to other people. If you play for their applause, you will crumble at their critique. The greatest leaders consider other people, but they don't cater to everyone. Leaders lead; they don't expect everyone to agree with everything they do, whether win or lose. Leading is hard enough without having to meet the changing approvals of a fickle audience.

CHAPTER 6

MARY, MARTHA, AND DABO SWINNEY

That's been my word all year, Love.

And I said it tonight, we're gonna win it

because we love each other.

—Dabo Swinney, Clemson University football coach[1]

Lie #5: Results are greater than relationships.

In January of 2017, the Clemson Tigers won the College Football Playoff National Championship. Pause. Let that sink in. I love the sound of it. My favorite team won! As a young kid, I can remember watching football games in the Clemson Tigers' home stadium, Death Valley, in South Carolina. I remember rubbing Howard's Rock. I remember the homecoming parades and tailgate parties. I will never forget meeting "The Tiger" and getting my picture with him, the sounds of the band when the team scored a touchdown, or singing "Tiger Rag." I bleed orange and white.

On January 9, 2017, I decided to throw a viewing party to watch the championship game. It was my wife, our four kids, and about twenty other friends who wanted to watch the game. We had tons of food, and almost everyone was pulling for Clemson to win (except for a few people, which made everything much more interesting). We were gathered to watch the University of Alabama, who had previously won a staggering sixteen national championships, go head-to-head with our Clemson Tigers. We had one championship to boast of …

Danny Ford.

1981.

Respect.

I remember listening to all the pregame reporters on ESPN talk about how great Alabama was and how powerful a dynasty they had built. Coached by the legendary Nick Saban, they were a powerhouse program who consistently landed the top high school players in the country. Many of those players would end up winning titles and then have successful careers in the National Football League. They were the most elite program in the land, dominating the college football landscape for over five years.

Anyone who knows anything about college football knows that 'Bama is simply the best. Numbers don't lie. Clemson, on the other hand, was coached by Dabo Swinney, one of the youngest college coaches in the game but who had actually played college football as a walk-on at Alabama. He didn't just play; he won a championship there as a player. Coach Swinney was now leading Clemson and building a growing program with far less experience but lacking nothing in heart. It was your classic David-versus-Goliath story, and the battle was about to go down in front of almost twenty-six million people tuning in to watch it live. The game would live up to every ounce of the hype it received.

I remember the excitement of kickoff and watching the entire first half of play. Though no one at our watch party was saying it for fear of jinxing the team, I believe we were all thinking the same thing: *We actually have a chance to win this game. Like, a real chance!* Clemson was playing almost to perfection while Alabama looked, well, vulnerable. They looked like a team that could be beat. It seemed, for the first time in a long time, we actually had the better team, or at least the better players. We most definitely had *the* best player. His name? *Deshaun Watson.* Deshaun was a Heisman finalist with ice running through his veins. Always cool. Always calm. Always collected. He guided the Tigers from the quarterback position throughout the entire game. With only two minutes remaining, Watson led the Tigers on a nine-play, sixty-eight-yard drive that ended with Watson throwing a touchdown pass with only one second remaining. One second. I can still feel the house shaking. We celebrated so hard the TV stopped working. We shook the cables loose from the television. We didn't care. It was over. We had won.

The real formula for Clemson's success takes place behind

the scenes. It takes place in the conversations most of us will never see the transcripts of. It takes place in small towns across the South and on road trips in the off-season. It takes place during phone calls and emails we will never know about. All those touchdowns you see on Saturday actually begin with conversations that take place on somebody's couch. Dabo Swinney is one of the best college football recruiters in the nation. In fact, he might be *the best*. For the past ten years, Swinney has consistently landed some of the top prospects in the nation. Not just the top, but the tip-top. Five-star recruits. The best at their positions.

It takes a special swag to be able to walk into a living room, look parents in the eyes, and convince them to send their son to your school. He is asking parents to entrust all the hard work and investment in their son into his program. These players are not just coming to play football; they are committing to give their lives to his program for up to five years. They're placing their future in his hands. The amount of trust, transparency, and relationship this takes is beyond comprehension for most people. Yet Dabo, somehow, repeatedly seals the commitment, and everyone ends up winning. Clemson gets a stud. Stud gets a scholarship. Parents get peace of mind. Everyone wins. In fact, the wins have just continued to pile up in the decade since Dabo took the reins at Clemson.

Over 130 wins.

Six ACC Conference titles.

Eight ACC Atlantic Division titles.

Three appearances in College Football Playoffs.

Two National Championships.[2]

Winning has become so common that now the top players in the country are actually begging to get into his program. How has he pulled this off? What is the secret?

Relationships.

Clemson is a family. Swinney says it all the time. When he recruits players, he invites them to join his family. Will they be playing football? Absolutely. But they will also be coming over to his home for dinner. They'll be invited to church with him. They'll know his wife and they'll be friends with his kids. They will band up with the other brothers on the team and be held accountable while being encouraged. Any time you hear Dabo Swinney talk about his coaching staff and players, he emphasizes the culture of family and relationships. The relationships in his program provide the power to overcome and achieve the desired result. He has found the key to success comes from the following reality:

Relationships matter more than results.

Relationships were the focus of Dabo's speech during the post-game celebration after winning the championship. After listing off what seemed like his entire coaching staff and members of his family, he gave this response to ESPN reporter Sam Ponder when Sam asked what he was feeling in those moments:

> It's indescribable. You can't make it up, only God can do this. Take a guy like me, from Pelham, go to Alabama, win a national championship, come to Clemson and have a chance to win a national championship against the best team in the country up until the last second of this game. And to see my guys fight, and just believe. … I told them that the difference in the game was gonna be love. That's been my word all year, love, and I said tonight we're gonna win it because we love each other. I told them at halftime that we're gonna win the game. … I don't know how, but we're gonna win it. It doesn't even seem real to me. It's been an unbelievable eight years.[3]

I know it's rare to hear a head coach credit love for winning a national championship, but you have to remember that Dabo Swinney isn't just any old coach. He has ambition that is strengthened by humility. He doesn't let pride convince him that results matter more than fostering relationships with his team.

As leaders, we have a natural ambition to do whatever we need to do to achieve our goal and make our dream a reality. Ambition is natural and healthy, but when it's influenced by pride, ambition can keep you from your most important mission, which is to love. Pride will cause you to buy into the lie that results matter more than relationships.

People matter more than your product, your profits, or your performance. And while all of those things definitely matter, the key word to remember is *more*. Results do matter, but relationships matter *more*! Whether you're a pastor, a coach, or a CEO, your success is most likely measured by what you do more than who you are. The "scoreboard" of your success tends to be the influence of your church, the number of wins you get each season, or your company's profit margins. Many times, this scoreboard is created and imposed on you by other people in your industry or even by public perception. And whether you like it or not, there is a tendency for us, as leaders, to naturally begin measuring our success based on these metrics. Before you know it, you end up leading an organization that tends to value results over relationships. And these stories never end well. But when we temper our ambition with humility, like Dabo Swinney, we can achieve the success we desire without using people in the process.

There's a story in the Gospel of Luke where Jesus Himself highlighted this very principle. He was traveling between two cities and decided to stop and spend some time with a few friends at their home. Even though Mary and Martha invited Jesus to come inside and hang out, they were not fully prepared for His arrival. At least Martha wasn't. Like many of us would, Martha sprang into action and began cleaning the place up. She fixed the throw pillows on the couch, put up the laundry on the table, and began to cook dinner for this special, but spontaneous, occasion. She was in full-tilt OCD cleaning mode while her sister Mary just sat in the living room talking with Jesus.[4] If you've experienced a similar situation (minus the part about Jesus being your guest), you know how infuriating this scenario can be. Martha was busting her tail to create the best possible experience for Jesus while Mary was just sitting down. But in the process, Martha was missing what was most important: spending time with Jesus. Luke makes it a point to tell us, "Martha was distracted by all the preparations that had to be made."[5] In other words, she was more interested in what she was doing for Jesus rather than in being with Jesus.

Eventually, Martha got so upset that she power walked into the living room and called her sister out. "Jesus, don't you even care that my sister has left me to serve alone? Tell her to come help me." I can just feel Mary's humiliation in this moment. She just got called out in front of the Son of God! This was a good old-fashioned sister showdown, and Jesus was sitting right in the middle of it.

Jesus' response here is a memorable one. As leaders, we always place a high priority on getting things done and getting better. That is our job: to make people better, make organizations better, and make communities better. We will always value those who do over those who don't. However, Jesus was profoundly clear in His response to Martha that relationships always matter more than results. He looked back at Martha, I think with a smile, and said, "Martha, Martha, you are worried and distracted by many things; but only one thing is necessary; for Mary has chosen the good part."[6] Basically, He told Martha that her priorities were in the wrong place. Rather than serving and working and focusing on results, she should have placed priority on her relationship with Jesus.

I can envision the confusion on Martha's face ... and maybe even your face right now, because this runs counter to almost everything we have ever been taught. We are the ones who do more than others, grind harder than others, work the longer hours, and have the whatever-it-takes mentality. The idea that Jesus would encourage sitting and having a conversation while there are things that need to get done? Absolute blasphemy! However, He says point-blank that our relationship with Him is more important that anything we do for Him. I believe that this principle of relationships applies to our everyday lives.

As I reflect on the past twenty years of my life of work in church ministry, I have seen this principle of valuing relationships play out in both positive and negative ways. I have celebrated with some of my closest friends as they experienced great success in their churches because they valued relationships and loved people well. I have also spent countless hours counseling other friends of mine who, in prideful ambition, treated people poorly and almost lost everything in the process. They fell into the trap of caring more about results, such as church growth and numbers, and began to use people as a platform for their personal ministry to stand on. They lost their churches, their influence, and in some cases, their families.

Before I expound more on this issue, it is important to acknowledge that this is a temptation for any and all of us. Whether you're a pastor like me or a parent obsessed with grades, if you emphasize all of your energy on results over relationships, you'll eventually end up losing both. The truth is this: if you're a leader in any capacity, there will always be the temptation to use people more than love people because loving people is much harder. It requires more time, effort, and persistence. Don't take the easy way out because it always ends tragically.

Some may think this technique is a soft or weak approach to business. I get it, because I once thought the same thing. For the vast majority of my life, I believed the best picture of great leadership was a five-star general with a perfect physique and a flawless image. I envisioned him standing up on a platform before a vast army of people. He was the epitome of excellence and demanded the same from everyone under him. He was strong, firm, and driven to the max. His standards were strict, and he screamed success and victory no matter the cost. To me, this was an ideal picture of leadership. I wanted to be just like the general. A platform, a podium, and thousands looking on in admiration. I've said it before and I'll say it again: pride can poison even the best of intentions. Prideful ambition can often lead to performance mentality. Performance promises that you'll get medals and stars based on what you do, not who you are. Therefore, the more you do, the more you are. This is the standard for most companies, teams, and organizations. Churches, too. However, it is a dangerous and destructive paradigm for everyone involved, and it is time to make a change.

Unfortunately, I carried this performance mentality into my own journey when planting a church. I was driven, passionate, and ready to change the world. There was nothing I could not do, and I believed, much like a general, I was on my way to engage in upcoming "battles" that would eventually bring victory, whatever the heck that meant. I led with a chip on my shoulder and surrounded myself with a small team of people who operated the same way. I saw obstacles as opportunities and faced challenges with tenacity. I banned words like "can't" from my vocabulary. I was tough as nails and resolute that the way I was doing things was right. This was my flawed understanding of leadership, and I expected those I was leading to live and lead with the same edge. This caused many tense conversations and a production pace that almost led to personal burnout. While these characteristics are not naturally harmful, they can be prioritized in a way that can lead to unnecessary harm. Focusing on results will inevitably lead you to walk over people, while valuing relationships will enable you to walk with people. I can promise you from personal experience that walking with people is much more effective and fun. Walking over people is not only uncomfortable and painful but it makes the journey unstable and unpredictable.

Over the past seven years, our church has become one of

the fastest-growing churches in our state. What began with just nine people in a living room has grown into a thriving, multi-site church. At the beginning of each year, we get letters and emails from our state convention informing us we are leading in church attendance, baptisms, and overall growth. While there was a time these letters acted as a sort of "badge of honor," I can honestly say that they reflect and resemble so much more at this point in my journey. Now, when we receive these letters or reports, we do so with gratitude because we know that, ultimately, God is the one to thank for establishing something so pure and powerful.

We've seen tremendous growth over the years, and looking back reminds me that it is nothing short of a miracle. The results we are experiencing are amazing, and many people center their celebrations on just that: results. Their prideful ambition blinds them from the real feat: a movement fueled by love. When I consider all we, as a church, have seen and celebrated, I'm reminded that the foundation of it all is the people. The root of it is relationships. And the guarantee of our future success is founded on the very principle that Jesus Himself established ... love God and love people.[7] Period. Do the results matter? You bet they do. But do people matter more? Absolutely. I've just learned that when you truly focus on the relationships, the results will eventually come. However, if you focus primarily on the results, your relationships will most definitely go. Check your priorities.

Truth #5: If you value relationships, results will follow.

Ambition turned prideful causes you to believe the lie that results are greater than relationships, and this limits your team from reaching their full potential. Humble ambition means prioritizing relationships and ensuring your team thrives.

LEADING THROUGH THE LIE

As you begin to consider the impact of focusing on results within your sphere of leadership, start with expectations. In leadership, there should always be a balance between setting clear expectations and inspecting outcomes to ensure that expectations are met. Valuing relationships is not a "pass" on addressing poor results. It's quite the opposite. When you truly value relationships, it means that you use results not as a weapon to cause strife, but rather as a tool to shape and craft your team to achieve your desired outcomes. As you take this approach, your team will see the difference and rise to accomplish greater results. Here are three powerful ways to implement a relationships-greater-than-results mentality.

1. *Value people for who they are and not just what they do.* Rather than operating with a performance mentality, consider a different approach that emphasizes relationships. Get to know your team. Who are they and what makes them tick? What are their favorite foods, sports teams, music genres, or vacation

spots? Take some staff retreats or casual days. Ask questions about their families and get to know their kids' names. It's amazing what happens when you build relationships with those you're trying to build a vision with. This will not happen accidentally; it happens intentionally. And, because you're a great leader, you already know how to do this well. Map it out, create a plan, and see how positive the shift is over the next few weeks.

2. **Praise in public; critique in private.** Let the whole world know the praises you have for someone, but save the developmental conversations for your private office one-on-one. This will communicate a high value of relationship with your team while also ensuring that you address shortcomings in pursuit of better results. By caring about both in a healthy balance, you will communicate to your team that relationship with them matters more.

3. **Treat them the way you want to be treated.** This is, in essence, loving them well. It's what most of us grew up hearing as the Golden Rule: "Do unto others as you would have them do unto you." Jesus said it like this in Matthew 22:39: "Love your neighbor as yourself." And by "neighbor," He meant everybody. While it can be easy to forget this in the stress of day-to-day interaction, it's important to remember. The

way you treat your team will be the way they treat theirs. This ripple effect sets the perception of how people see your organization and, by correlation, how they see you. As you seek to love and serve people well, you'll discover that love truly is the secret sauce to strong and successful relationships.

CHAPTER 7

MAKE A WAY, NOT AN EXCUSE

Nobody wants to show you the hours
and hours of becoming.
They'd rather show the highlight
of what they've become.
—Angela Duckworth, *Grit*

Lie #6: I don't have what it takes.

"To launch a successful church, you're gonna need somewhere between $150,000 to $200,000 in the bank." What? I know. Trust me. I couldn't believe it either. I heard this while sitting in a large room at the Exponential Church Planting Conference in Orlando, Florida. This conference, consisting of over five thousand church leaders from around the world, is the mecca of church planting and is *the* place for networking, resourcing, and attaining guidance on how to be successful in launching a healthy and thriving church. I've attended every year for the past seven years because it is three full days of celebration, inspiration, and motivation to fulfill the dreams that God has called me to carry out alongside thousands of other dreamers. I have discovered on this journey that dreamers fuel dreamers. Vision feeds vision. If you don't have a place like this to go, find one that suits your field. You'll be better for it. But I've also found that sometimes vision can be terrifying and big dreams can be frightening.

On that day during the conference, I got a taste of that brutal reality. When I heard how much money I needed to launch a "successful" church plant, I cringed and felt my spirit cower back. I heard a voice in my ear whisper, *You don't have what it takes.* I became anxious. I tensed up. I looked around to see how others were responding to this news and began to feel insecure and insufficient. I feared I had led my team, my family, and even my young church to evident failure. What leader does that?

Was I actually trying to fail?

Was I just too idealistic?

Maybe I was just too impatient?

Would we even make it this month?

How are we making it all?

I was just told that I needed $200,000 in the church bank account and we had … $6,500.

Six thousand five hundred dollars.

I reflect back on that moment and I can distinctly remember laughing. You know, like one of those "Come on, man … you gotta be kidding me" type laughs. The kind that results from disbelief in what is being shared and your mind simply can't comprehend it. Laughing was my coping mechanism to cover up my fears. I wanted the guys on my team sitting with me to feel confident in *our* plan rather than the plan that "has worked for hundreds of other churches." However, I knew we were out of our league with those figures. We had already started having weekly church services, so it was too late to go back. Fundraising six figures of support just didn't seem possible. I felt stuck between a rock and a hard place as a leader, while at the same time feeling an odd sense of accomplishment. Although those feelings of fear crept in, a spirit of faith quickly trampled them. Maybe, just maybe, there was something instilled deep down within my soul that refused to buy into the lie that says **I don't have what it takes.**

Let me explain.

I grew up broke in a town called Bishopville. It's a blue-collar town in rural South Carolina where cotton fields span for miles and there are only a handful of grocery stores … and even fewer stoplights. I was raised by a single mom along with my two sisters after my parents divorced when I was young. Some of my fondest memories are playing Barbies on the side screened porch with my sisters (don't judge!) and walking to the end of our street to Pizza Hut to play music on the jukebox. I spent my days building forts in our backyard, climbing trees, and riding bike trails through the woods with my friends. While it wasn't a booming metropolis with tons of opportunity, it was a great place for an adventurous boy to grow up with few boundaries and familiar streets. The only concern we ever had in those days was the Lizard Man who haunted our town and the entirety of Lee County. If you want a good rabbit trail conspiracy theory, just go Google that; the Lizard Man of Lee County. Bishopville provided a great place for me to spend my childhood days. But Bishopville was also more than that; it became the breeding ground that planted the seeds of grit and grind of the builder I've become.

My parents divorced when I was just a kid. I have no recollection of the divorce, and one of the greatest testimonies to my parents is that I have no memories of any stress or fighting between them. I just know things didn't work out and they went their separate ways. What this scenario meant for me was that I was raised by a single mom who was in way over her head. Though she was young, beautiful, and full of life, she was solely responsible to provide for and raise three kids under the age of seven. This presented some major challenges for her. She had no college education, no corporate career experience, and no time to go and actually pursue those things. However, groceries had to be bought, bills had to be paid, and her kids needed a consistent anchor called Mom in their lives. There was too much to do and too little time to do it.

Among all the childhood memories that stand out to me, one is a trip we took as a family to the local grocery store. I would often volunteer to accompany Mom to the grocery store just so I could ride on the buggy and buy bubble gum at the checkout. Occasionally, I would get the privilege of picking out some snacks and throwing them into the cart. On this day, I grabbed some Twinkies and hoped I could slide them through the checkout. I remember getting to the checkout lane and helping put the groceries up on the belt. As the cashier scanned each item, I hoped with all my heart that Mom wouldn't tell me to put the Twinkies back. Thankfully, they made it past her and into the pile to be put into the paper grocery bags. It was always my job to help bag the groceries as my mom settled up payment for the haul. As I was stuffing the bags, my mom was talking with the cashier. They were discussing what items were "allowed" to be purchased with the food stamps program we were on.

For as long as I could remember, we had used food stamps to buy groceries each time we'd come. I just thought they were coupons. This was our norm. However, today was different. I watched them go through the bags and pull out certain items. I remember the feeling in my heart and in my soul when my Twinkies got pulled out. *No!* I thought. *Take the eggs or the toilet paper ... just not my Twinkies!* I remember looking at my mom and seeing her tear up. Like, real tears. I had seen her cry before, but never at a grocery store. Never like this. This was different. It felt different. And that's because it was.

My mom was desperate.

And I've discovered in life that desperate people do desperate things.

And, every now and then, desperate people do amazing things.

My mom decided she wanted a better life for us. She somehow knew if she caved to the circumstances in front of her, things would never improve. While there were many hardships and difficulties in her life, she refused to play the victim, and she made a decision to begin building the life she wanted. She reached out to a local college and went through the application process to start her education. She had no way of paying for it, but it didn't matter. According to most people, she didn't have what it took. But she knew she had to make a way. Desperate people do. People with grit do. She got accepted and started classes. I still can feel the excitement I had for her when she told us she was going back to school. With no way to pay for it, no plan to finance it, and no idea how many challenges would face her over the next few years, this single mom with three kids started her freshman year of college.

During the daytime hours she went to class while we all went to preschool and grade school. In the afternoon and evening hours, she would turn our home into a daycare, providing after-school care for other kids while their parents worked. This helped provide financial resources to pay for bills, rent, and groceries. It allowed us to keep our home and have a sense of stability even during long seasons of uncertainty. Each night after dinner, Mom would buckle down with her books and study. I can still see my mom with her stack of books on our couch in that little house, and I'm still amazed how she carried it all. For three years, she devoted herself wholeheartedly to her education, and she made a way. God provided everything we needed in those years, and Mom is quick to give Him all the credit. While I fully believe God did provide, I also believe God expects us to put our hands to the plow and embrace the work in front of us. God doesn't bless lazy. I watched my mom grind, sweat, and sacrifice to achieve a Bachelor of Science in Education and become a middle school teacher. It was 1988 when she finally got through, and I can still picture her bright, white smile on her graduation day. She did it. She made it. Against all the obstacles and against all the odds.

That's what hustle looks like.

That's what building looks like.

A whole lotta faith and a whole lotta fight.

〽️

One of the greatest leadership books of all time is found in the Bible; it's titled Nehemiah. The setting is seventh-century BC Babylon, where the Israelite people had been in captivity because of their disobedience to God. The king of Babylon was Artaxerxes, and he had a faithful Israelite cupbearer named Nehemiah.[1] Basically, the job of a cupbearer was to eat or drink anything before the king to ensure it wasn't poisoned or contaminated.

The cupbearer was the test; if the meal was poisoned, he died.
You can only imagine the level of loyalty and trust in a position
like that.

One day, Nehemiah received word that Jerusalem, the capital
city of his native country, was in ruins. The walls had been torn
down, the city had been destroyed, and even though the Israelite
people were starting to rebuild, their spirits were demoralized
because their city was demolished. Nehemiah heard this report
and immediately became burdened by it. He knew he had to do
something, but he didn't know what exactly. He sat on the issue,
prayed about it relentlessly, and felt compelled to approach the
king with a request. Here he was, the most trusted man in all
the kingdom, and he was about to ask the king for permission
to leave. Nehemiah had nothing of his own; all he had was the
king's. His clothes, his room, his food, his wealth, his job …
everything, and he was about to walk away from it all. It made no
sense, unless you've ever received a calling and burden like this
from the Lord. Nehemiah had, and he decided to make his move.[2]

Nehemiah went to King Artaxerxes and shared his burden
for Jerusalem and his desire to go and rebuild the walls and the
city. He made some major requests of the king by asking for both
protection in his travels and provision to help rebuild the walls.
The king granted him permission and gave him everything he
needed for the journey. Nehemiah then stepped out and made his
way to Jerusalem. By combining strategic leadership and divine
vision, Nehemiah and his workers rebuilt Jerusalem's walls in just
fifty-two days. The people could return to the city.[3] God blessed

His people, and Israel began to reclaim their identity and culture that had been taken away. All of this happened because one man decided to walk in obedience toward a burden God placed on him to carry. Nehemiah decided that even though he had nothing, he would do something and trust God to come through on his behalf. He refused to buy the lie that he didn't have enough, but rather chose to step out in faith and trust God in the process. I'm convinced if we want to experience the same kind of success, we must be willing to do the same.

When I heard I would need $200,000 to start a successful church, I began praying that God would provide. I was working a full-time job during the week while also trying to get our new church off the ground. I prayed that God would give us financial partners to support us in our work so some of the stress would be relieved and I could devote more time to ministry and leadership. I watched the very next week as God answered that prayer in two very specific ways:

- A church contacted me saying they wanted to get involved in the great work God was doing. They wrote us a check for $24,000.

- A church-planting network reached out wanting to partner in our mission to reach the city of Charleston. They wrote us a check for $36,000.

In just a matter of days, our account had grown from $6,500 to $66,500, a 1,000 percent increase, almost overnight! I was blown away! In addition, calls began coming in from other pastors and churches saying they had heard about our story and wanted to partner with us. Checks started arriving in the mail, long-term financial partnerships developed with multiple churches and networks, and when our first full year of ministry was completed, we found ourselves in a healthy financial place to provide for our needs while giving generously toward other missions as well. Throughout the story of Awaken Church, God has always come through. He has always provided for our every need. I refused to believe the lie that **we don't have what it takes** and chose instead to look forward in faith that God would provide what we needed. Because the reality is this: if we're committed to the fight and we're willing to have some faith, we will always have enough.

When pride poisons grit, we start believing the lie that we don't have what it takes to achieve our dreams. We get scared that we won't be able to accomplish our dreams even if we try, so why try? We believe it would be worse to try and fail than not try at all. And that's simply not true.

I think those early days of my childhood were preparing me to be a church planter and pastor. I think those days of growing up laid the foundation for me to become a leader. Being broke showed me how to become a builder. There will be challenges to anything worth achieving. Your ability to assess those challenges and determine a way forward will be the key to your team's success. There will always be someone or something that reminds you of your lack and leads you to assume you don't have what it takes to move forward. You have to push back against that lie and remember why and how you started in the first place. Grit is about having the faith to fight for your dreams and goals. Remember the dream and remember the risk. Remember the faith and remember the fight. Remember your resolve to make a difference, no matter what other people had to say. That mentality has to be there. And stay there. You simply cannot cave to the echoes that say you don't have enough. Because the truth is, you do.

You always have and you always will.

Truth #6: You have what you need; it just takes grit to find it. With grit, you have what it takes to overcome any obstacle that stands in the way of your dreams. If you're committed to the fight and can find a little faith, you will always have enough for what it takes!

LEADING THROUGH THE LIE

Think about the last big decision you didn't capitalize on. Maybe it was a new program you wanted to launch. Perhaps it was a product line you hoped to create. Maybe it was a tournament you backed out of or a hire you backed away from. What has kept you handcuffed from capitalizing on opportunities?

As you ponder these questions and consider the people you are currently leading, establish these practices to overcome the dangerous lie that **you don't have what it takes.**

1. *Establish your faith and find your fight.* Do you believe in your mission? When you believe in what you are working toward and have a cause bigger than yourself, then you are able to fight for your mission. Without faith, you'll lose your fight, and you'll start believing you don't have what it takes.

2. *Break the problem down.* When I realized I was at least $100,000 short of what I needed, I was overwhelmed. We can't let obstacles blind us from our dreams. What is the obstacle clouding your vision? After you identify it, break it down into small steps you can take to overcome. I reached out to people, called potential investors, and asked other church leaders for fundraising tips. The only way to climb a mountain is one step at a time.

3. *Celebrate often.* When we dig deep, find our grit, and work toward our goals, it will be hard, but we will eventually achieve victory. It is crucial to celebrate the small victories along the way, even before the big victory is won. Take the time with your team to celebrate each and every milestone that gets you closer to achieving your dream.

CHAPTER 8

POWER IS NOT THE PROBLEM

It's sort of a lonely job.

—Tim Cook, CEO of Apple[1]

Lie #7: It's lonely at the top.

Leaders are powerful people. There is an assumed measure of power and control that comes with being looked to as someone with influence. As leadership expert John C. Maxwell famously stated, "Leadership is influence; nothing more and nothing less. And influence … well, influence is a really big business."[2]

The digital world of social media has fueled the rise and prominence of *influencers*. An influencer, by definition, is someone who has influence over a large group of people. In the same way, advertisers have used athletes and celebrities to promote products for decades (think Gatorade using Michael Jordan in their "I wanna be like Mike" campaign). Influencers are more of a modern-day, organic method to use people with notable platforms to leverage their power to influence other people's decisions. The most successful influencers on social media platforms such as TikTok or Instagram make over six figures a year as they promote products from clothing to cars. Elite influencers with more than a million followers can rake in over $250,000 for a single sponsored post! The reason this avenue of marketing has become such a big business is because if you can leverage someone's influence to inspire and attract people to your product or service, you win. Influence is an incredibly powerful and profitable resource, and it needs to be managed well. Power is a peculiar thing. Some people selfishly seek it out while others wake up one day and realize they have it.

My guess is that you didn't set out with aspirations to be in some powerful position; most leaders don't. But over time, as the business, ministry, network, or program grew, you inevitably began to take on greater responsibilities and gained influence. As influence grows, power grows with it.

The most powerful people in the world are often the loneliest people, or so we're told. There's an old proverb that states, "It's lonely at the top." We have been fed this idea that seems to equate great leadership to climbing a mountain. The weak fall away or die off while only the strongest and greatest ascend to the summit. Few make it to "the top," so it becomes lonely up there. But what if this isn't true? What if it is a lie we've been fed, shaping how we conduct ourselves? What if the loneliness at the top is not some guarantee of success or result of power, but rather an indicator of our own ideals? In other words, what if those leaders who are lonely have actually decided they *want* to be lonely? That would also mean that if leaders wanted the "top" to be a little more crowded, we have the power to create that outcome as well, right?

I think so.

We must first understand how power changes people. It changes leaders. This is scientifically true. Power has been proven to pervert the psychological processes that nurture close relationships and healthy connections with others.[3] The science behind this phenomenon is fascinating. As leaders begin to accumulate influence and power, their natural response to others' words and actions change.[4] Actions that were once seen as merely generous gestures begin to create a sense of paranoia about being manipulated. The leader starts to believe that every conversation or decision made by a team member inherently comes with an ulterior motive. They believe that, because of their power and position, they have become a target for those around them seeking only selfish advancement. This leads to an undermining of trust and, ultimately, a disconnect from many of the same relationships that helped them achieve the very success they currently have. Because trust has been jeopardized in these relationships, the leader begins to pull away and isolate with a sense of self-preservation and a desire to not disappoint. This does not make the leader bad so much as it makes them normal. Again, there is an ample amount of psychology and science to support this scenario. The leader becomes incredibly lonely and disconnected from their team and organization over a period of time. The top becomes a lonely place, and they have no idea how to get back down. This scenario is where the vast majority of leaders find themselves today.

Isolated.

Alone.

Misunderstood.

They don't want it to be this way.

And it doesn't have to be.

While power perverts and distorts a leader's outlook, there is a contrasting element that can drastically change an individual and organization: **empowerment.** Merriam-Webster defines "empowerment" as "the act or action of empowering someone or something: the granting of the power, right, or authority to perform various acts or duties." In other words, it means sharing or redistributing one's power to allow others to gain position or influence. And it is hard to find a better example of empowerment than Martin Luther King, Jr.

As one of the most celebrated leaders of all time, Dr. Martin Luther King, Jr. was a Baptist minister and social activist who led the Civil Rights Movement in the 1950s and 1960s. As an African American raised in the segregated rural South, he faced uphill battles his entire life. Growing up in the inner city of Atlanta, King found school to be easy but church to be difficult. He was uncomfortable with religion and could not reconcile his faith with being looked down upon and being treated unjustly as a young Black man. In his junior year of high school, he became serious about his faith and determined to make a positive difference in the world around him. King graduated from high school and went on to earn a degree from Morehouse College, then Crozer Theological Seminary in Pennsylvania. It was during his college years at Morehouse that racial injustice and inequality became the nation's paramount issues, and he knew he had to help lead the change. After graduating from seminary, King moved back to the South and spent years engaged in civil rights activism in Birmingham, Mobile, and Atlanta. He became the prominent leader and face of the Civil Rights Movement, which lasted from 1954 to 1968.[5]

The most fascinating aspect of King's leadership was his ability to empower those around him. While he was definitely the most influential Black man in the United States at the time, he had a unique ability to cast vision and distribute his power to the millions rallied around him. One of the most profound examples of empowerment can be gleaned from his "I Have a Dream" speech, delivered during the March on Washington in 1963. It was there, on the steps of the Lincoln Memorial, that King addressed over 250,000 people to deliver the most iconic speech in modern history.

And so even though we face the difficulties of today and tomorrow, I still have a dream. It is a dream deeply rooted in the American dream.[6]

I have a dream that one day this nation will rise up and live out the true meaning of its creed: "We hold these truths to be self-evident, that all men are created equal."

I have a dream that one day on the red hills of Georgia, the sons of former slaves and the sons of former slave owners will be able to sit down together at the table of brotherhood.

I have a dream that one day even the state of Mississippi, a state sweltering with the heat of injustice, sweltering with the heat of oppression, will be transformed into an oasis of freedom and justice.

I have a dream that my four little children will one day live in a nation where they will not be judged by the color of their skin but by the content of their character.

I have a *dream* today!

I have a dream that one day, *do*wn in Alabama, with its vicious racists, with its governor having

his lips dripping with the words of "interposi-
tion" and "nullification"—one day right there
in Alabama little black boys and black girls will
be able to join hands with little white boys and
white girls as sisters and brothers.

I have a *dream* today![7]

If you've never listened to that speech in its entirety, you
should. The passion, vision, and sheer resolve in his voice is an
inspiration to this day. It was a pivotal example of leadership
because on that day, over 250,000 people embraced his pro-
claimed vision and became empowered to move to action to
achieve it. King wasn't standing alone on top of that summit that
day; he was surrounded by an army of advocates that he chose
to bring along for the journey. He wasn't isolated and alone; he
was supported by more people than you or I could ever imagine.
That is what good leadership looks like. That is what the top can
look like. That is how it can be different if you refuse to buy into
the lie that says loneliness accompanies great leadership. That is
what happens when you shift from being a leader who *has power*
to being a leader who *empowers*. It changes everything.

King had such a profound impact on racial equality and
justice that he saw the passing of the Civil Rights Act of 1964,
authorizing the federal government to desegregate public spaces.
Later that year, King would win the Nobel Peace Prize at the
young age of thirty-five, a remarkable feat. And though he was

tragically assassinated only a few years later, his legacy and leadership lives on to this day. The reason? **Empowerment**. Rather than hoarding his influence or using his power for personal gain, King willingly gave it away and, in the process, empowered millions of people to change history for the benefit of generations to come. And we're all better for it.

$$\bigwedge$$

Empowerment can be scary because it involves entrusting power to another person or group of people. There is always an inherent risk involved. Any time you give power away to someone, they have the ability to use it against you. But the reward usually far outweighs the risk. Is there a chance you will get burned in the process? Of course. Even the best leaders have been betrayed or backstabbed. But the chance that you'll see your people empowered to rise in success is far greater than the risk and most definitely worth it. I have personally seen the positive impact of this life-changing principle through the life of one of my closest friends, Jeff Cook.

Jeff is the founder and owner of Jeff Cook Real Estate, one of the fastest-growing and most successful real estate companies in the United States, number ten in the country, to be exact. Since 2003, when Jeff started the company, JCRE has seen growth at a rapid pace. Dozens of agents were hired, trained, and equipped to sell homes and make families' dreams come true. Jeff became Charleston's leading real estate agent in 2011 and has held that title every year since. The company has successfully expanded beyond its main headquarters in Charleston to new offices and representation throughout the entire state of South Carolina. Jeff Cook Real Estate was among the top twenty-five fastest-growing companies in South Carolina, and in 2019 was named the Top Workplace in the state, as well. Perhaps the most impressive aspect of their success, however, is the commitment to Jeff Cook Cares, a charitable arm that funnels revenue back into efforts to improve the city, state, and even the world. Whether it's paying for hundreds of pet adoptions at the local animal shelter, providing backpacks full of school supplies to hundreds of students at low-income schools, or building homes internationally for families in Haiti or Peru, Jeff models both grind and generosity as well as any leader I have ever known.

So, what's the secret to his success? There are more than two million real estate agents in the United States, so why aren't they all experiencing the same results? Is it because Jeff is in the hottest market? Is it because he recruited the right people? Is it because he worked harder and invested more hours along the way? Some of those may have been contributors to his success, but as I have witnessed over the past decade, the ingredient that comes to mind when examining his success is simple: empowerment. Jeff has recruited, developed, and deployed over 400 real estate agents through the years and has helped them establish successful careers while meeting the needs of thousands of families each year. His ability to empower his agents has created a company that runs itself with smoothness and effectiveness.

And, there isn't a better example of this pipeline of development and empowerment than the story of Bryan Wilson.

Back in 2003, Jeff was a top salesman for the retail giant Circuit City. His manager at the time was a man by the name of Bryan Wilson. Bryan was a very successful business manager who himself was building a great career within the commercial retail industry. His job was to recruit, train, and develop salespeople to build a high powered team that increased bottom line profits. It was his very focus and intensity that helped him develop team members like Jeff who eventually became a sales leader for the entire company. The strategic system was working well, and sales were thriving. However, corporate businesses can often be brutal, and even the best in the business sometimes pay the price. In the end, the company decided to make cutbacks, and Jeff got caught in the crossfire. His manager, Bryan, broke the news to him, and that was the day Jeff began to pursue his dream in real estate. Though Bryan remained at Circuit City, he kept up with Jeff and watched from a distance as his former salesman began to make his mark in the real estate world. Little did he know they would reunite someday.

Fast forward a few years later to 2016 when Jeff Cook Real Estate was booming. While selling hundreds of homes each year, there became a significant need for increased leadership within the organization to sustain the growth that they were experiencing. Bryan Wilson, who had been watching this company grow from the outside, decided to reach out to his former salesman and pitch a novel idea: to join forces again. Bryan came on board as a real estate agent with JCRE. He quickly became familiar with the real estate profession and was soon selling homes with the best of them. The same principles of leadership that made him successful in retail were now helping him build a career in real estate. The only difference was that he was now part of a company that entrusted and empowered him. At JCRE, Bryan is rewarded with success and not merely being used to bring success to some corporate bottom line. This process of empowerment has positioned him to be one of the most trusted members of Jeff Cook Real Estate as he now oversees and leads the original office location in Charleston.

Jesus set examples of empowerment all throughout His earthly ministry. This leadership trait is one of the most defining characteristics of Jesus' ministry, yet the people called to follow His example often overlook it. Think about this: there has never been a more powerful person to walk the planet. Jesus **was God** in the flesh, meaning He was both fully human and fully divine. This is why He was able to give sight to the blind, make the deaf hear, make the lame walk, and walk on water. He didn't simply exist in creation; He was over all of creation and had the power to do whatever He wanted. He carried all authority in heaven and on earth, but rather than hoard that power and use it for His personal gain, He chose to use His power to equip other people and change their lives for good. By doing so, He developed and empowered a small band of followers to go change the world.

The Gospel accounts are full of stories where Jesus empowered people just like you and me to do world-changing acts. The one story that jumps out at me is the moment recorded in the book of John when Jesus was teaching on a hillside by the Sea of Galilee. Thousands of people had come to hear this popular street preacher explain the mysteries of the kingdom of God. They came from towns and cities all around the region and spent hours leaning in and listening to this man who claimed to be the Son of God. As the day went on, the people must have become hungry and started to complain. Maybe His disciples were just worn out from keeping crowd control in the heat for all those hours. Either way, as the sun was going down, the disciples came to Jesus and said, "Look … everybody's hungry. It's time to call it a day. Let's dismiss all these people so they can start heading home and find themselves some food on the way." Keep in mind that there were 5,000 men at this conference, though most scholars agree there were over 15,000 people because women and kids would not have been included in that count. Without even blinking an eye, Jesus responded by saying, "They don't need to go anywhere. Y'all just give them something to eat." Jesus must have been preaching up a storm because He was on a roll and wasn't quite ready to wrap this thing up, or maybe Jesus just had something else in mind to put an exclamation mark on this incredible occasion. Either way, the disciples were stunned and confused because they didn't have a buffet ready to feed a crowd that size. In fact, all they had was a lunchbox some kid had brought with only five loaves of bread and two fish in it. When Jesus saw what they had to work with, He confidently said, "That'll do, boys."[8]

He instructed the disciples to divide the massive crowd into smaller group sizes of fifty and one hundred. Then Jesus prayed over the small portion of fish and bread in that lunch box, and God miraculously began to multiply it. Jesus had His disciples find baskets to distribute the food. Just imagine the back-and-forth trips that the disciples made getting their baskets filled with food from Jesus and then walking throughout the crowd and distributing it among the people. These disciples were getting to experience the people's extreme gratitude while carrying out Jesus' ministry at a very real and practical level. Meanwhile, Jesus was down by the water doing the hard work of multiplying the meal so the magic of ministry could take place. In all reality, He was working behind the scenes and the disciples were the ones on the front lines getting the accolades and appreciation. That is what empowerment looks like.

It should come as no surprise to us that these same disciples would go on to lead the early church movement following Jesus' death, burial, resurrection, and ascension back to heaven. They continued to preach in the streets, build culture-changing communities, carry out ministry to widows and orphans, and perform life-changing miracles. They invited other people to join them in the movement and helped to develop and empower others.

This intentional empowerment created the global phenomenon we now know as the Church. It's a movement that has spanned for almost two thousand years while involving billions of people along the way. The Church is a powerful movement that has touched almost every corner of our planet and included all ages, races, ethnicities, and backgrounds. It has delivered countless benefits to society such as orphanages, adoption, education, abolition of slavery, medicinal advances, hospitals, prison reform, serving the poor, and the list goes on. The Church has shaped governments, penned policy, and brought peace in an otherwise unstable world. This movement that has helped humanity in countless ways was only made possible because of the way Jesus leveraged His influence—or should I say power—to truly empower others.

> **Truth #7: The true measure of power is how many others you empower. When power is corrupted by pride, you become calloused and your team suffers. When you choose to use your power to empower those around you, you have a much greater impact on the world than you could have had on your own.**

LEADING THROUGH THE LIE

Think about the people who have empowered you along the way. Maybe it was a coach who let you call the plays as the game was winding down. Maybe it was a boss who empowered you to make real decisions even though it cost both time and money. It may have been a parent who entrusted you with responsibility or a boss who passed the baton of leadership. We have all personally experienced some form of empowerment, and it is time we started sharing that feeling with those around us.

Take a few moments to contemplate the influence or power you have as a leader in your organization. Now consider those around you or under you. Can you see how much leadership potential exists in the room around you? The only thing they need to rise is for you to start investing your power into them. Here's a few practical ways to start empowering your team and experiencing true growth toward success.

1. *Identify growth tracks for the entire organization.* Think about each person in your organization and what their path to success looks like. Whether they are the receptionist or the chief financial officer, every person on your team should have a next step in their personal growth and development. Take time to process what the growth track is for each person and position on your team. Write it down, make it known, and provide the tools and resources necessary for those next steps to be taken.

2. *Create a mentorship mentality.* Everybody should have a shadow; somebody watching what they do and learning how to do it. This pipeline of mentorship will not only train the next generation of

leadership in your company or team but will also enhance the quality of relationships. This mentoring will allow the maturity and experience of more seasoned employees to be shared with newer employees, creating unity and building confidence.

3. ***Share the spotlight.*** Bad leaders ask other people to lead the things they don't personally like doing. Average leaders ask others to lead things. Great leaders ask others to do the things that they love doing. Be a great leader. Choose to let others on your team enjoy the opportunities that you love as a leader. Bring them on the work trip that may have perks and benefits. Let them speak at the company-wide party or do the interview for the local news station. Share the spotlight and give away the glamor of leadership whenever possible and watch the return on your empowerment and investment.

CHAPTER 9

THE CHOICE THAT CHANGES EVERYTHING

We change our behavior when the pain of
staying the same becomes greater than
the pain of changing. Consequences give us
the pain that motivates us to change.
—Dr. Henry Cloud & Dr. John Townsend, *Boundaries*

As a leader, you are probably very familiar with change. It's what you do. It's who you are. You live to change lives, minds, and the very industry you're in. You have learned to embrace change. You adapt strategies, expand services, shift structures, and change communication. You've scaled your business model, your leadership team, and possibly every aspect of your life. As a leader, you exist to lead change in all areas. So with this truth, why is the hardest person to change **you?**

There is a high probability that after reading this book, you will realize you need to change some things. No one likes to be told that, but chances are, you already know you need it. As a leader, you already know the areas of your life where you are crushing it and doing well. You are also aware of the areas in life where you struggle and keep hitting a wall. As you read this book, there's a good chance that many of those areas have been exposed for the first time. You've come face-to-face with the reality that one of these lies has haunted you for a long time and you may feel paralyzed on how to move forward. That's normal. And I can tell you I have been there before. It is hard to go back and address an issue that has been present for years. And it is humbling to admit you don't know it all or that you have even contributed to the chaos in your team or organization. However, as a leader, choosing to accept this responsibility and change is the only way things will improve. There is immense growth and success that takes place when you bury your positional pride and rise up as a renewed, relational leader. I am not suggesting that this choice is easy, and I'm definitely not saying it's fun. It is, however, a choice that must be made if you are going to move toward and experience the success that is waiting on the other side.

In order to experience true change and greater success, you will need to assume a posture of hunger and humility. Humility is a character trait embraced by the greatest leaders, but it is not a trait that takes shape overnight. I have found that the character traits that make successful entrepreneurs and leaders are often the same traits that combat the characteristic of humility. Therefore, it is imperative that you seek humility as you would a treasure, because that's exactly what it is. It is not only a valuable trait for you and your team but it is a priceless trait that will transform your life. One of the greatest examples of humility is found in the greatest (in my opinion) sports movie of all time, *Remember the Titans*.[1]

Produced by Jerry Bruckheimer in 2000, *Remember the Titans* is based on the true story of a Virginia high school football team that miraculously banded together during the forced integration of their school in 1971. In summary, a white school and a black school were thrown together and forced to figure out everything, including the assimilation of academics and athletics. Amid the struggles this created for everyone involved, the movie captures the journey through the lens of the T.C. Williams High School football team, better known as the Titans.

The entire plot of the movie thickens when Coach Herman Boone, played by Denzel Washington, is selected to become the head coach for the Titans. The school board made this decision in an effort to calm rising racial tensions in the Black community. This move forced the existing head coach, Bill Yoast, to step down into an assistant position. Obviously, this decision did not sit well with the white community or Coach Yoast himself. Despite his initial decision to step away from football altogether,

Coach Yoast decides to remain on staff as the Defensive Coordinator under Coach Boone. With this move, the racial tension is at an unprecedented high when training camp opens up and school begins. The players hate each other, the coaches hate each other, everyone is on a side, and it appears that the entire effort to integrate this community will eventually result in disaster. However, the movie chronicles the exact opposite as the football team ultimately joins together and paves the way for the entire community to do the same. The racial reconciliation and healing that takes place is led by the efforts of both Coach Boone and Coach Yoast as they work through their differences and inspire their team to follow. While there are dozens of leadership lessons within the movie, there is one particular scene that stands out to me.

When the Titans advance to the 1971 Virginia State Championship, they find themselves struggling in a game that matters more than any other. Coach Yoast has lost his best defensive player, Gary Bertier, to a car accident and finds himself unable to adapt his strategies to stop the opposing team from advancing. His team is getting trampled on, and it appears he does not know what to do. The crowd is going wild, the emotions have all peaked, and it seems that everything they have worked for all season is now on the line. It is in this moment that Coach Yoast does the unthinkable …

He walks over and asks Coach Boone for help.

Actually, he asks Boone to take over.

Earlier in the season, Coach Boone had been questioned about his defensive strategies. In a heated game with the season on the line, Coach Boone walked over to the sideline and asked Coach Yoast, "What are you doing, Coach?" In football terms, this is a subtle way of saying, "You don't know what the he** you're doing!" No man wants to hear that question, so Yoast responded the way most any leader would. "You just worry about your offense and I'll worry about my defense." Once again, in football terms, this means, "Shut up and back off." This moment magnified the reality that although these two men both coached the same team, they were about as separated and aggravated as you can imagine. There was zero teamwork between them, and the idea of giving or sharing ideas for improvement was the last thing on their minds. They survived that game, but now they were at the big state championship.

The game-changing moment came when one leader made the decision to ask for help and accept the help. And this required humility.

Coach Yoast asks Coach Boone to take over the defense.

Coach Boone takes over the defense.

The Titans go on to win the game.

They become the 1971 State Champions.

〰️

As you consider what changes you would like to see take place within your team, your business, or your organization, it's important to remember that it all starts with you. That's what leadership is. **You go first**. And in order to change as an individual, humility has to take over. You have to admit those areas of your leadership where you've embraced the lies and shift your current beliefs to embrace the truth instead.

For instance, if you have bought into the lie that *results matter more than relationships* but you now see the value of relationships first, you must first own that mistake and seek to make personal changes before attempting to implement the idea professionally. Since we know our beliefs ultimately drive our behaviors, it is imperative that your personal beliefs begin to change your behaviors. Otherwise, you run the risk of implementing change out of convenience, not conviction.

Once you are personally walking out these truths, then consider involving your team in a collaborative session to discuss potential changes for your team or organization. One of my favorite exercises as a leader is to engage in honest feedback with my leadership team in a "speak free" format. In this exercise, my leadership team is allowed the opportunity to critique, analyze, give feedback, and have a conversation about the issues we are dealing with internally as an organization. While this time is always guided with integrity and honor, it allows a space where true dialogue can occur without fear of reprimand, should disagreement be present. I encourage you to create a similar space. By creating this type of collaboration and discussion, you will be best equipped as a leader to contemplate strategy on how to implement change. Once decisions are made, you will discover increased morale and overall engagement helps positive and lasting change take place, benefitting everyone involved!

Finally, let me encourage you to make the choice to rise above the lies that all leaders face. It is a choice only you can make.

Choose to push back against the negative mindsets that have shaped your organization.

Choose to stop believing things will just always be the same old, same old.

Choose to deconstruct your values and build them back stronger.

Choose to reflect personally and do the work to get better.

Choose to challenge the status quo of settling in place.

Choose to embrace humility over pride.

Choose to serve others, not just lead them.

Choose to get better every single day.

Choose to rise above the lies.

There are so many people who are waiting on you to rise up. Your spouse. Your kids. Your friends. Your teammates. Your staff. Your leadership team. Your customers. Your community. Your world. I want to remind you of the reason you got into all of this in the first place. You had a dream, a goal, and a vision to change the world. My hope and prayer is that you still do. After all the grind, the hustle, the good times, and the bad times, the truth is people still need you. We still need your heart and passion to change peoples' lives, and the principles outlined in this book will help make that happen. I know you want to succeed and I know you want to grow; if you didn't, you wouldn't have picked up this book. Now I want you to find the spark that ignited your dream in the beginning and start fanning that flame until it's roaring again. There is so much more to be done, and you have what it takes to make it happen.

As you rise above the lies and see leadership from an entirely new perspective, know that your greatest days are ahead of you and the best is yet to come!

ENDNOTES

Chapter 1

1 Genesis 3:1

2 Genesis 3:4-5

3 See Genesis 3

4 See 1 Kings 4 and 10-11

5 Proverbs 16:18

Chapter 2

1 Nietzsche, Friedrich. *Basic Writings of Nietzsche*. Translated by Walter Arnold Kaufmann. New York, NY: Modern Library, 1968.

2 Hebrews 11:6

Chapter 3

1 See Exodus 14-16

2 See Exodus 18:13-16

3 Exodus 18:17–23 MSG

4 See Exodus 18:24

5 See Exodus 19

Chapter 4

1 Quote found in: Campbell, David J., David Edgar, and George Stonehouse. *Business Strategy: an Introduction*. Basingstoke: Palgrave Macmillan, 2011.

2 "Who We Are." Chick. Accessed November 30, 2020. https://www.chick-fil-a.com/about/who-we-are.

3 "Focus on Getting Better...a Leadership Lesson from Chick-Fil-A and Andy Stanley - Flock:Ology." flock, October 7, 2010. http://www.flockology.com/2010/10/focus-on-getting-bettera-leadership-lesson-from-chick-fil-a-and-andy-stanley.html.

Chapter 5

1   Blodget, Henry. "Check Out This Awesome Michael Jordan Quote About Success..." Business Insider. Business Insider, November 3, 2011. https://www.businessinsider.com/michael-jordan-success-2011-11.

2   See John 13:38

3   See John 18:15-18

4   See John 21:15-19

5   Matthew 16:18 NASB

6   See Matthew 27:3-5

7   "48 Famous Failures Who Will Inspire You To Achieve." Wanderlust Worker, November 6, 2020. https://www.wanderlustworker.com/48-famous-failures-who-will-inspire-you-to-achieve/.

Chapter 6

1   Hood, David. "Love. Legendary. Two Words That Led to a National Championship." TigerNet.com. TigerNet.com, July 25, 2017. https://www.tigernet.com/story/Love-Legendary-Two-words-that-led-to-a-National-Championship-16028.

2   "Clemson Tigers Football." Wikipedia. Wikimedia Foundation, November 8, 2020. https://en.wikipedia.org/wiki/Clemson_Tigers_football.

3   Hood, David. "Love. Legendary. Two Words That Led to a National Championship." TigerNet.com. TigerNet.com, July 25, 2017. https://www.tigernet.com/story/Love-Legendary-Two-words-that-led-to-a-National-Championship-16028.

4   See Luke 10:38-42

5   Luke 10:40

6   Luke 10:41–42 NASB

7   See Matthew 22:36-39

Chapter 7

1   See Nehemiah 1

2   See Nehemiah 2

3   See Nehemiah 2-7

Chapter 8

1   "Tim Cook, the Interview: Running Apple 'Is Sort of a Lonely Job'." The Washington Post. WP Company. Accessed November 30, 2020. https://www.washingtonpost.com/sf/business/2016/08/13/tim-cook-the-interview-running-apple-is-sort-of-a-lonely-job/.

2   Maxwell, John C. 2007. *The 21 irrefutable laws of leadership: follow them and people will follow you.* New York, NY.: HarperCollins Leadership.

3   Inesi, M. Ena, and Adam D. Galinsky. "Five Reasons Why It's Lonely at the Top." The Wall Street Journal. Dow Jones & Company, March 25, 2012. https://www.wsj.com/articles/BL-SOURCEB-22878.

4   Robertson, Ian H. "How Power Affects the Brain." How power affects the brain | The Psychologist. Accessed December 7, 2020. https://thepsychologist.bps.org.uk/volume-26/edition-3/how-power-affects-brain.

5   King, Martin Luther, and Clayborne Carson. *The Autobiography of Martin Luther King.* London: Abacus, 2006.

6   "'I Have a Dream," Address Delivered at the March on Washington for Jobs and Freedom." The Martin Luther King, Jr., Research and Education Institute, January 25, 2019. https://kinginstitute.stanford.edu/king-papers/documents/i-have-dream-address-delivered-march-washington-jobs-and-freedom.

7   "'I Have a Dream," Address Delivered at the March on Washington for Jobs and Freedom." The Martin Luther King, Jr., Research and Education Institute, January 25, 2019. https://kinginstitute.stanford.edu/king-papers/documents/i-have-dream-address-delivered-march-washington-jobs-and-freedom.

8   See John 6:1-13

Chapter 9

1   Yakin, Boaz. 2000. Remember the Titans. United States: Buena Vista Pictures.

ABOUT THE
AUTHOR

Brandon Bowers is the founding and lead pastor of Awaken Church in Charleston, South Carolina. One church with multiple locations, Awaken started with nine people in a living room and has grown into a vibrant movement of 'seeing people far from God awakened to life in Christ.' Brandon holds a Master's Degree from New Orleans Baptist Theological Seminary and serves as a leadership catalyst for multiple ministry networks. He and his wife, Ashley, have four children and live in the Charleston area.